T0194255

Learning to Slow the F*ck Down

and other life lessons

Erica Mortimer

BALBOA.
PRESS

A DIVISION OF HAY HOUSE

Scriptures taken from the Holy Bible, New International Version®, NIV®. Copyright © 1973, 1978, 1984, 2011 by Biblica, Inc.™ Used by permission of Zondervan. All rights reserved worldwide. www.zondervan.com The "NIV" and "New International Version" are trademarks registered in the United States Patent and Trademark Office by Biblica, Inc.™

Balboa Press books may be ordered through booksellers or by contacting:

Balboa Press
A Division of Hay House
1663 Liberty Drive
Bloomington, IN 47403
www.balboapress.com
1 (877) 407-4847

Because of the dynamic nature of the Internet, any web addresses or links contained in this book may have changed since publication and may no longer be valid. The views expressed in this work are solely those of the author and do not necessarily reflect the views of the publisher, and the publisher hereby disclaims any responsibility for them.

The author of this book does not dispense medical advice or prescribe the use of any technique as a form of treatment for physical, emotional, or medical problems without the advice of a physician, either directly or indirectly. The intent of the author is only to offer information of a general nature to help you in your quest for emotional and spiritual well-being. In the event you use any of the information in this book for yourself, which is your constitutional right, the author and the publisher assume no responsibility for your actions.

Any people depicted in stock imagery provided by Getty Images are models, and such images are being used for illustrative purposes only. Certain stock imagery © Getty Images.

Print information available on the last page.

ISBN: 978-1-9822-1049-6 (sc)
ISBN: 978-1-9822-1052-6 (hc)
ISBN: 978-1-9822-1051-9 (e)

Library of Congress Control Number: 2018909868

Balboa Press rev. date: 08/17/2018

Contents

Introduction

Every day, I am learning to live my truth.

—Erica Mortimer

This book was created after Patty Gianotti, a therapist who works for me, looked me straight in the eye and said, "Erica, you have to help women." Her words struck me. I think I may have even gasped. Her words struck a chord within me; they resonated as true within my spirit. It was in that instant that I realized I needed to step out of my comfort zone and take some big risks. I knew it was time to come out of the shadows and stop hiding. I knew I needed to be a vessel for something bigger, something beyond me and what I could even imagine. But first I needed to be willing to become vulnerable in a way I hadn't done before.

So here is the truth—you and I aren't that much different. It doesn't matter what part of the country you're from or how you were raised. We are alike. We rush through life putting others first and not taking care of ourselves. We are afraid of change, of being alone, of living, of loving, of embracing the power within us.

Most of the ideas in this book have naturally developed as themes in my own life. In my years of of working with others, I noticed I wasn't alone. The things I personally struggled with were the same challenges others struggled with as well. I have compiled what I believe to be a few life-changing topics. Well, they were life changing for me anyway. I consider myself a professional student. I'm constantly in pursuit of knowledge, understanding, and growth. I have embraced a double mission of sorts. I spent years on this quest to heal my wounded spirit and continually work to know my "true self"—all while trying to figure out new ways to help those who are silently suffering and are still lost. Throughout the process of writing this book, I compiled much of what I have learned from the works of great authors and spiritual leaders, including the guidance of gifted life coaches and other teachers God has strategically placed in my life. Someone once said, "No man is your friend, no man is your enemy; every man is your teacher."

Family members are often the greatest teachers, and I may have had some of the best. Born into an Italian family and raised in Trenton, New Jersey, I went to Catholic school, made my first communion* and confirmation, had pasta with my Nona* on Sundays, corrected my mother's English, and sat on plastic-covered sofas. Like most Italian-American kids, I was "beat" with a wooden spoon. I was taught to fear my parents, the nuns—those in authority; and I was taught to fear getting hurt both physically and emotionally. I was taught to be quiet, obey without question, and be a good girl. I remember in third grade that other kids talked about what their parents would do if a teacher ever hit them. Unsure what my parents would do in that situation, I thought it would be a good idea to ask my mother. So that same day, I went home and asked my mom what she would do if a teacher hit me. Her response was, "I'd give you the beatin' of your life, because you must have done something to deserve it."

I knew better than to act up. My parents always seemed to know what I was doing and where I was. There were consequences for not being "perfect" and not saying the right thing, doing the right thing, sitting still when I was supposed to, and moving when I was supposed to.

My fear of authority was reinforced at school. I was scared to death of the nuns. Since they had finally stopped hitting kids, they turned to humiliation as their preferred form of punishment. One boy who was caught chewing gum had to put the gum on the end of his nose and keep it there for the rest of the day. In the first grade I remember that a boy farted, and the nun made him stick his head out the window. I know—it makes no sense. She should have made him stick his butt out the window, but these nuns made no sense. They were unpredictable and always angry. In those days, it seemed that the best thing to do was to be quiet and not be noticed. To stay within the parameters set for my life, I learned to stay safe, play small, and hide. Those who didn't get noticed didn't get in trouble.

Never happy, my parents were always at war. They finally divorced as I was going into high school. With no clue of how to love or who to love, I was married by the age of twenty-one and had two children by the age of twenty-eight. Looking back, I can see how fear drove the decision to get married, and fear of loneliness drove my decision to have children. Ultimately, it was fear that kept me in a loveless relationship for eleven long, unhappy years. I felt alone, frustrated, and stuck. My loneliness later turned to bitterness and a brewing anger. I felt the venom within me growing. After my divorce, I went from one unhealthy relationship to another, always settling and never finding love.

I had grown to be cold, hardened, and guarded—some would say standoffish. I was so numb and shut down that I was convinced I didn't have the capacity to love anyone, including myself. Maybe I didn't give love a chance. Maybe my walls kept everyone and everything, including love, out. Maybe my fear of being alone interfered with my vision. Or maybe feeling unworthy of love overshadowed all else. Looking back, I know I chose fear over love. I chose to rush into things rather than to patiently wait for God to bring the right person into my life. I always chose to be with the wrong person rather than to stay with myself. Ironically, it was my fear of being alone that kept me isolated and lonely.

Starting around the age of sixteen, I knew I wanted to help people, but that desire was about all I knew. I had no direction or clue of what I wanted to do with my life. I later studied psychology at Clemson University and then received a master's degree in school and community mental health counseling at the University of South Florida. I have been working in the field of mental health since my first job as a mental health technician at the age of eighteen. I worked in a home for the elderly who were severely mentally ill. The people I worked with suffered from severe and debilitating mental illness, which included schizophrenia, bipolar disorder, psychosis, and obsessive-compulsive disorder. I remember one older gentleman who was admitted into the home after he castrated himself. Yikes! I typically covered the overnight shifts.

One night while doing my rounds, I found a patient sitting at a table by herself, making motions that looked like she was dealing cards. I remember asking her what she was doing, and she said she was playing poker with Jesus and the Holy Spirit. All I could think to say was that I didn't think Jesus gambled. Her witty response was, "He sure took a gamble on you." These patients gave me a run for my money and provided the best introduction to the field of mental health. I later worked in juvenile prisons and schools, always able to reach those who seemed the most difficult, resistant, and "lost." As a high school guidance counselor, I found more joy in working with the special education students and those with behavioral issues than with those striving to get into an Ivy League school.

In what I can explain only as a God thing, I left my comfortable tenured position as a public school guidance counselor and opened a drug and alcohol treatment center called Center for Healing. Looking back, I shake my head and say to myself, "It is crazy what you can do when you start trusting God." I had no confidence, business experience, treatment experience, or any clue what I was doing. I took life one day at time, as they say, and committed myself to trust God. When life felt like it was going sideways, I woke up and just prayed. I distinctly remember my prayer; it went something like this: "Hey, God, I was thinking. Maybe you should lead today, and I'll follow. When I try to lead and wait for you to follow, it doesn't seem to go so well." I found that I created only a mess when I tried to force things to happen. If you have a chance, listen to Carrie Underwood's song "Jesus, Take the Wheel." That song sums up how I was feeling.

The old me had some very bad habits that needed breaking. I had a pattern of reacting before I had all the information. I had the habit of expecting the worst and always planning for failure. I had the habit of looking for the bad in everyone and everything. I could always find a problem or something wrong to focus on. If I couldn't find something wrong, I made shit up in my own head. It was as though I were always looking for a reason to be angry. Maybe I was just trying to justify how I felt. I had the habit of wasting enormous amounts of time and energy creating backup plans for when things would go wrong. I even made sure I had escape routes for my backup plans. Oh, and I also had the habit of running—from people, challenges, and uncomfortable situations. I was running from feelings. I was running further and further away from my true self. If you keep running, not knowing where you are going, you will eventually be lost. I *was* lost. I had no idea who I was or what I was capable of doing.

Today my life is very different. I love challenges, and I face them head-on. Today I'm able to slow the fuck down. Today I take care of myself physically, emotionally, and spiritually. I'm not afraid of failure; I now see failure and mistakes as opportunities to grow. Things I once found difficult I now find to be effortless. Today I choose to find the good in every situation, and I choose to approach life from a place of gratitude. There is no room in my life for bitterness and anger. I choose joy.

The life I live today wouldn't be possible if I had continued living my life of rushing around, not feeling, and being terrified. You know what they say. "If you always do what you've always done, you'll always get what you've always got." I went from living what I considered to be a very vanilla life to one that is more like the greatest ice cream sundae you have ever had in your life; any flavor of ice cream—with sprinkles, caramel sauce, peanut butter, chocolate sauce, anything you like—you can have.

My friend said to me the other day, "You do the coolest things." I laughed and said, "You wouldn't have said that five years ago." Today I try new things. I run my own business. I have an awesome team of employees. I have great friends who inspire me, push me, and encourage me in every area of my life. I have amazing kids. And I am also blessed with an amazing, hardworking, loving husband, who supports even my craziest ideas. I can honestly say that I finally know what love is. I can finally say that I am never lonely. I can finally say that life is good and exciting. I am never bored, and I never create backup plans. And by the way, I am still learning to slow the fuck down. Today I recognize areas of my life where fear still roars its ugly head, but I no longer let fear drive my life. Fear no longer dictates my future.

This book is intended to help you see how I went from being a wreck and spinning out of control to living a life beyond my wildest dreams. It's my desire that you will learn to slow the fuck down and get to know your true self—that you recognize and overcome fear, that you move past the roadblocks that are keeping you from abundance, beauty, pleasure, joy, and all that is yours by Divine right.

And as my sister goddesses say in response to a voiced desire, "And so shall it be or something even greater beyond your wildest dreams."

About This Book

Iuse the terms *God*, the *Divine*, and the *Universe* loosely and interchangeably. I have profound respect for all religions, but I don't subscribe to just one. I find great wisdom all around me and in many forms.

When you see an asterisk (*), you can go to my website and see a picture that relates to what I'm talking about. Just go to EricaMortimer.com.

I find healing in music, so I may reference different songs. It would make me happy if you jotted down the song names and listened to them later.

And just remember, I'm talking to you as a friend.

Chapter 1

Slow the Fuck Down

Speed is irrelevant if you are going in the wrong direction.

—Mahatma Gandhi

Learning to slow the fuck down was the only way writing this book was even possible. My old way of thinking would have prevented me from even attempting to write this. The conversation I had with myself would go something like this: *It would be so cool to write a book and share what I have learned over the years.* Then I would think, *Never mind, that will take me forever.* Anything that required time and patience or seemed to involve a lengthy process wasn't an option, as far as I was concerned. I was impulsive, and I wanted quick results.

For example, after graduating from Clemson, I knew I wanted (needed) to get a master's degree in counseling. I knew it would be a three- to four-year process: take the GRE exam, apply, wait to hear from the Admissions Department, and then actually get through the program and internship. Who has time for all that? I used to say, "I would love to do it, but it's such a lengthy process." One day I woke up and realized I had been using the same excuse for not working toward this dream for four years. Yes, four years!

I could have completed the program in the time I had wasted by making excuses. If only I had just done it and stopped complaining about how long it was going to take. Looking back, I know fear also played a part in my decisions to put off the application process. Fear of failure held me hostage and prevented me from initially applying.

We live in a fast-paced era. Everything is about convenience and immediate satisfaction. We aren't forced to wait for much—not like when I was growing up. If you are close to my age, you may remember how long it took just to call your friend. You had to go home or find a pay phone and have enough change with you just to be able to make a call. Then you had to find the friend's number in an actual address book or on a slip a paper if you didn't have the number memorized. In my house, we didn't have one of the fancy phones with push buttons; we had a rotary phone. Heaven forbid you had to dial a number that had a bunch of eights in it. You had to wait for the dial to slowly come all the way back around before you could dial the next number. I still remember my home phone number from when I was a kid (888–4351). Nowadays, the only phone number I have memorized is my own. Everyone I speak to regularly is on speed dial or on my favorites list on my iPhone. I have grown to like life as it is today—quick and easy. I got to where I wished there was a speed dial for everything in life.

I'm not sure where I got the drive to want to take over the world in a single day, but I did. I had somehow moved from not wanting to do anything due to fear of failure to wanting to do everything. Well, almost everything. If it was going to take a huge commitment or years to accomplish, then I wasn't interested. But if I could get it in place in the next month or so, that would be fine. To be honest, I think my attempt to stay busy was merely a distraction from the personal chaos I was living. I was in turmoil. I looked like I had my life together, but honestly I was depressed, lonely, and lost. Staying busy gave me something else to focus on so I didn't have to face what was really going on in my life. Staying busy protected me from feeling. Rather than sit in my personal pain—or better yet, deal with it—I was busy dancing around the issues that haunted me daily.

Looking back, I was basically rushing to remain average, doing nothing well. I had the focus of a puppy bouncing from one thing to another. I know now that there is a false sense of accomplishment that comes with staying busy, constantly doing, and always striving.

There are moments in our lives that stand out as pivotal turning points. These moments don't always make sense when we're sitting in the middle of them, but looking back, we gain clarity. I see now what I didn't see then. Like you, I have had a number of these moments. One stands out and has become the basis of this book.

Several years ago, I traveled to Florida for work. I always make a point to visit one of my colleagues who owned a treatment center. (I hadn't started Center for Healing at this time in my life.) The first few minutes of every conversation were always the same. He would ask what I had been up to since we last talked, and I quickly and excitedly rattled off a list all my innovative ideas and projects I either was working on or wanted to work on. From there, our conversations went like this:

> Sherief (leaning over his desk with authority, looking me straight in the eye, piercing my soul, and speaking slowly): Erica, slow the fuck down!
>
> Me (squirming in my seat): I know, Sherief; I am.
>
> Sherief: You don't know. To know and not do is to not know. *Slow the fuck down!*

I wish I could say I had understood the first time and that we had that conversation only once. But that isn't the case; we had this same conversation countless times—pretty much every time I saw him. I guess I never really understood what he was saying. I thought I did. At the time, I couldn't see what he was seeing. I couldn't see that I had set myself up for failure time and time again. I couldn't see that I was creating more chaos. It was only after I learned to slow the fuck down that I understood what he was talking about. I hadn't spoken to Sherief in years, but last year, I called him and thanked him. I told him that I finally understood what he had been saying.

While learning to slow the fuck down, there came a newfound awareness. Slowing down allowed me to look within. Previously, my focus had always been external. This awareness was more of an awakening. And it didn't happen overnight; it has been a process that has taken place over several years and hasn't ended. This awakening started as I began to understand meditation and mindfulness, which were such foreign concepts for me that I had a hard time wrapping my head around them. For me, there was nothing natural about either meditation or mindfulness. I remember one of my coaches telling me to take five minutes and pay attention to the spaces between my thoughts. My reaction was, "What the fuck? Are you kidding me? My thoughts have thoughts. There are no fucking spaces!" I began to notice that I was thinking several thoughts at the same time.

My brain was always in overdrive. It was like a three-ring circus in there. Thoughts swirled through my head every waking moment. I'm not even sure that my brain took a break at night. It was hard for me to fall asleep because of my racing thoughts. When I did fall asleep, it was common for me to wake up in the middle of the night with what I thought to be another great idea. My head was so filled with my own chatter that there was no way to get still and quiet. Noticing the spaces between thoughts wasn't an approach to mindfulness that was going to work for me, so I had to work to find strategies I could effectively use. Sometimes the only thing I could do was just breathe and pray. Prayer seemed to be a way to control (or at least organize) some of the noise in my brain. I guess you can call my prayers focused or more intentional chatter. I even began journaling to slow and control the flood of thoughts that rushed through my head.

I began searching for ways to quiet the noise in my head. I was desperate to find someone who knew how to meditate and had specific instructions on how to achieve mindfulness. I wanted the process spelled out for me. I found that several of my friends were already practicing meditation, so I asked them lots of questions, but no one could give me the answer I was looking for. I wanted a recipe. I wanted to hear steps one, two, and three. I wanted directions such as "Get on one knee, say the Hail Mary five times, and toss salt over your shoulder while singing, 'Hallelujah.'"

You see, I was a very literal kind of person. Remember, I was trained to follow rules; I didn't understand vagueness. I remember when my kids were babies, and the doctor said I could give them food. I wanted to know exactly how much and at exactly what time of day I should feed them. The doctor's vagueness drove me crazy. The thought of feeling my way through anything wasn't something I understood. My brain would robotically respond, *Does not compute.* I used to totally overthink everything in my life. I was looking for a clear set of directions or for someone to tell me the secret to getting quiet. If I didn't have a map, I wasn't going.

One friend told me he used this cool app called Headspace. He told me that meditation had drastically improved the quality of his life. He didn't need to convince me; I already knew I needed what meditation had to offer. Headspace wasn't a spiritual meditation, but it was clear and simple; and it gave directions. It was what I needed to get started. I needed to be led; I needed to be talked through the meditations. It starts off by telling you to sit for just a few minutes and increases the time with each day you use the app. This was the start of my mindfulness journey.

What I learned is that the release of judgment is the first step for anyone interested in meditation, mindfulness, peace, or learning to be present. Don't judge your meditation as good or bad. There is no wrong or right way to meditate. You need to do what feels right, and you can't beat yourself up for having drifting thoughts. They call it a meditation practice, because it is something you have to practice.

You don't need to join an ashram and meditate for hours on end.

You can start with five minutes a day. If that is too much, try two minutes. If that's a struggle, start by taking five deep breaths, paying attention only to the air filling your lungs, and emptying your lungs. If you are stressed, angry, or anxious, you can release those feelings through meditation. It is a beautiful thing. As you release the air from your lungs, picture yourself surrendering the stress and/or anger you may be holding in your being. Picture yourself releasing anything that doesn't serve you through your breath. As you inhale, imagine yourself being filled with love and peace. Remember, this is a meditation practice. Just keep practicing, even when you don't feel like you're doing it right. You will find that your mind wanders, and that is okay; just gently bring your thoughts back to your breath.

As I have learned to meditate, I have learned to slow the fuck down. Through this practice, I have learned what it means to be present. I have also learned how to be intentional in my thoughts and actions. When I come from a place of intention, I am less reactive in everyday situations. This means I don't have to freak out over every little thing that doesn't go as planned. I can stand back and view the situation with calm and objective eyes. I can see it for what it is rather than seeing it as bigger than it really is. I can *choose* how I'm going to react. I can choose how I will handle a situation. I know now that I can choose not to react at all.

Owning a drug and alcohol treatment center, I know a lot of crazy shit happens. It used to be common for one of my employees (Cassie) to freak out about something stupid that just happened and expect me to get worked up as well. I learned to listen to her without reacting. I would let her explain the situation (and vent). I would ask a few questions and then just sit there. It looked like I was just sitting there, but I was just focusing on my breathing and considering all my options. After I talked Cassie off the ledge and came up with a viable solution, she and others asked me how I could stay so calm. My response was always the same: "What good will come from me getting worked up?" or "How will it make the situation better if I get

6

upset too?" They all now know that I refuse to match their energy. When I come from a place of reaction or emotion, I make impulsive judgments and bad decisions; I jump to conclusions that often aren't true. When you slow down, you have time to get all the facts. Half of the time, the situation Cassie was upset about wasn't even a real problem. The other half of the time, we found that Cassie didn't actually have all the facts, though in her panic she thought she did. It was usually a misunderstanding or just some drama a client was trying to create to distract us from other things he or she was trying to sneak by us.

How many times have we reacted and jumped to conclusions, only later to find out they were totally wrong? How much more peace would you have in your life if you didn't get upset by every little thing that didn't go according to plan? I can tell you that mindfulness has had a significant impact on the quality of my life, and I know it will change your life too. A fellow clinician once told me the following story:

> One of my patients who had severe psychosis had some moments of lucidity and asked me if I knew the difference between reacting and responding. I told him I thought I did but asked him to explain what he meant. He posed two scenarios. In the first, someone is lying in a medical hospital bed and had been given new medication to treat him or her. The doctor comes in and tells the patient, "You're reacting to the medication. Would that be a positive or negative thing?"
>
> My initial answer was, "Negative."
>
> In the second scenario, the doctor enters the room and says, "You're responding to the medication."

I told him I thought that would a positive thing. He smiled and said, "That's the difference. Meditation allows you to respond to life rather than to react."

Chapter 2

Mastering Stillness in Motion

In the midst of movement and chaos, keep stillness inside you.

—Deepak Chopra

I am not a fan of birds. To be honest, I am scared of them—not a little bit but a lot. Despite my terror, I am fascinated with hummingbirds. They have a quality I strive for; they have mastered stillness in motion. These tiny birds can flap their wings seventy times per second yet appear to do so with ease while hovering perfectly still. They symbolize the enjoyment of life and lightness of being. Wouldn't it be nice to develop adaptability and resilience while keeping playful and an optimistic outlook? These little birds represent the following:

- Independence
- Being more present
- Playfulness and joyfulness
- Rising above negativity
- Swiftness and the ability to respond quickly

- Resilience—about to travel great distances tirelessly and effortlessly
- A reminder to lighten up and drink deeply of the nectar of life

How about it? Wouldn't you like to be more like a hummingbird? Wouldn't you like to rise above negativity and taste the nectar of life? I love the idea of being still and moving at the same time. That is what I continue to strive to do in my life these days. I have learned that I can move forward in life, making progress, growing, and contributing, while remaining calm and coming from a place of purpose. Maybe it's a stillness of heart, a stillness of being.

There were times when my ambition and desire to achieve led to impatience, impulsivity, and poor planning. I have a tendency to bulldoze my way through life. I had the attitude that I would plow through and make something happen. I would do what I had to do to get something done quickly. I just figured I would resolve any issues as they arrived, and I usually did. I would fix whatever mess I created as I noticed it. I was always in reaction mode. I felt like I could never get ahead of my problems. My approach to life came with a price. Moving too fast, putting Band-Aids on problems that required surgery, and making impulsive decisions often resulted in chaos and complications. I may have achieved some of my goals but unusually not without a whole lot of drama. You know the expression "putting the cart before the horse"? That is basically how I went about life, trying to give the answer before I even knew the question. Literally. I had been known to try to give an answer even before the other person had finished asking his or her question. That behavior is pretty fucked up. You may have heard it said that others are just a reflection of ourselves. Basically, if there is something about another person that bothers you, you need to take a look at yourself.

I mentioned that Cassie was always worked up about something. You may have figured out by now that she is easily excited. My husband refers to her as a cartoon character.* Everyone who visits our office says she should have her own reality TV show. Cassie is really good at what she does, and she has a deep passion to help those who struggle with addiction, but she is hyper. She moves a hundred miles an hour, is a go-getter, is fiercely loyal, and also talks extremely loudly. Cassie is also someone who doesn't let me finish a sentences. She is always trying to guess what I'm going to say next and finishes my sentences for me, like she is doing me a favor. She does this even though she has no clue what I am about to say or what the topic might even be. This behavior drives me crazy. I end up yelling, "Would you let me finish what I was saying before you respond?" She makes serious conversations difficult, especially because I work with her, rely on her insight, and seek her opinion. I try to get her feedback, and there have been plenty of times when she gives me an answer to a question I wasn't even asking. Ugh.

Well, I have seen my reflection in her. I now make a conscious effort not to assume I know what the other person is about to say. I listen to hear and understand as opposed to listening to respond. Which is what Cassie does. She is so busy planning what she is going to say that she doesn't even hear me.

And just for the record, when I originally wrote this chapter, I didn't use Cassie's name. After reading the draft of this book, she called me, hysterically laughing and saying she knew I was talking about her and that I should have just used her name. So I did. Now she tells everyone I am roasting her, but we all pick on Cassie as if it were a sport. But we love her, and picking on her is so much fun and way too easy.

Sometimes the process of achieving your dreams takes time, patience, and stillness. If you keep digging up the seeds of your dreams or trying to rush the process, you just end up with a mess. This past summer, I tried to grow carrots for the first time. I was excited when I saw that the seeds I had planted were growing. As they grew bigger and bigger, I was eager to pick my prized carrots. I couldn't wait. I started pulling them out of the ground to check on them. I was looking for signs of progress. I knew they weren't ready to be picked, but I pulled them out anyway, reasoning with myself that I would just pick one to see how it was going. It drove me crazy that I couldn't see what was happening underground.

By the time the carrots were ready to be picked, there were very few left. I should have just focused on growing the garden, watering it, and pulling any weeds that might interfere with the growth. I could have used my time more wisely by doing a little research on the growth process of a carrot. Instead I took matters into my own hands and pulled them out of the ground. I know—it sounds like a really dumb thing to do, but that is honestly what I did. I should have trusted the process and allowed for the growth. It makes no sense to pull or harvest your crop before its ready. But we do it anyway. We quit too soon because we often assume nothing is happening just because we can't see the changes taking place. Or we try to speed things up. We want things to happen on *our* timeline, forgetting that there is a natural process for everything and that God's timing is perfect.

Mastering stillness in motion requires awareness. It requires us to slow down and get clear. As I became aware of my own lack of awareness and lack of presence, I was surprised by how much I was missing in life. It's crazy how blind I was. When I say "lack of awareness and presence," I'm talking about those situations when I'm not in the moment. Those are times when I'm physically present but mentally checked out, consumed by my active brain and overtaken by fear, anxiety (and sometimes depression) that acted as a barrier between me and the rest of the world. I was sometimes so consumed with the conversation taking place in my head that I missed pieces of the conversation with the person I was actually supposed to be talking to.

This experience is similar to when you are driving a familiar route and get to your destination without any memory of making the turns. You don't remember the journey. My chaotic brain kept me from enjoying what was in front of me. I was either engulfed with worry or already thinking about what I was going to do next. Early in my mindfulness journey, I had an experience that made me take a step back; it was one of those pivotal moments.

One day I wanted to go on a hike. I was looking forward to going and couldn't wait to get into the woods. I convinced my husband that he needed to come with me, that it would be fun. So off we went to the park. I probably took twenty steps into the park when I started thinking, *We should really hurry and walk faster so I can get back.* I started a list in my head of all the things I "had" to do: grocery shopping, laundry, cooking. I think I even started to convince myself I was either hungry or had an urgent need to pee. Maybe both. All I knew was that I needed to get back.

I realized it was common for me to miss moments because my brain was rushing ahead to the next perceived, critical thing on my to-do list. I could be excited about an event—I couldn't wait to get somewhere—but then I would get there and be ready to leave and go on to the next thing. I wasn't enjoying anything or anyone, for that matter. You know that expression—"Stop and smell the roses"? Well, most of the time I didn't even *see* the roses, so forget stopping and smelling them. I was so busy going and planning that I was missing moments. Why the hell was I always in such a rush?

As my awareness increased, I started to see the same frenetic energy in others as well as their lack of awareness. I recently started driving a Jeep Wrangler and learned about the "Jeep Wave." I didn't know this before, but when a Jeep (must be a Wrangler) passes another Jeep, the drivers wave at each other. I started to realize how often while driving I was totally zoned out. I would be driving along and suddenly come back to earth, thinking, *Oh no. How many people waved to me that I didn't even notice?* On the flip side, there are days when I'm totally on point and am waving at zombies, lost in their worlds. You know what I'm talking about; these are the same people who stand mindlessly in stores, totally unaware that they are blocking the aisle and holding everyone up. Or the people who don't see you and let the door close in your face. I'm not judging them;

I recognize they just aren't present. Most likely they are consumed with life.

When I'm present, I come from a place of intention. I don't get my feelings hurt as quickly. I am more balanced. I can be more objective and remember that not everything is about me. I find more joy in the day to day. I'm focused on the blessings of the moment. Today when someone responds to me in a way that is less than positive, I can take a step back and see that his or her response has nothing to do with me. I don't need to allow others to steal my light and joy. I can still smile, even when surrounded by negative people. Sometimes when I run into those who appear to be miserable, I don't avoid them; I try to engage them in conversation and see whether I can make their day just a little bit better. You don't know what others are dealing with daily. A little kindness goes a long way.

You might be surprised to see what happens when you respond to people with a smile. I have a little game I play. I find those who look unhappy, maybe a cashier or the lady at the post office (she always looks miserable). I try to engage them in conversation or make them laugh. If I can get them to crack a smile, I know my work there is done. When I know it's not about me, I can give the situation a different meaning.

Let's say someone says something unkind to you. How differently would you respond if you thought it meant that the person was having a difficult day rather than thinking he or she had a problem with you? If you think the situation is about you, I bet you get defensive and lash out at the person or maybe stew in anger. If you consider what may have happened to the person earlier in the day, wouldn't it be easier to respond with kindness? The difference is between looking at someone and thinking, *What a miserable bitch*, or thinking, *I bet life has beat that person up. Maybe he or she could use a little kindness today.* Maybe you don't think the situation has anything to do with you, but the actions of others easily annoy you. Are you yelling, "Asshole" at the guy in front of you, who didn't go when the light turned green? This little story by Stephen Covey, author of *The 7 Habits of Highly Effective People*, gives you an idea of what I'm talking about.

> I remember a mini-Paradigm Shift I experienced one Sunday morning on a subway in New York. People were sitting quietly—some reading newspapers, some lost in thought, some resting with their eyes closed. It was a calm, peaceful scene. Then suddenly, a man and his children entered the subway car. The children were so loud and rambunctious that instantly the whole climate changed.
>
> The man sat down next to me and closed his eyes, apparently oblivious to the situation. The children were yelling back and forth, throwing things, even grabbing people's papers. It was very disturbing. And yet, the man sitting next to me did nothing.
>
> It was difficult not to feel irritated. I could not believe that he could be so insensitive to let his children run wild like that and do nothing about it, taking no responsibility at all. It was easy to see that everyone else on the subway felt irritated too. So finally, with what I felt was unusual patience and restraint, I turned to him and said, "Sir, your children are really disturbing a lot of people. I wonder if you couldn't control them a little more?"
>
> The man lifted his gaze as if to come to a consciousness of the situation for the first time and said softly, "Oh, you're right. I guess I should do something about it. We just came from the hospital where their mother died about an hour ago. I don't know what to think, and I guess they don't know how to handle it either."

We can't possibly know what others are going through, but we can remember that everyone is dealing with life the best way he or she knows how. But you will find that when you treat others with love and compassion, regardless of what you see, you will find that love and compassion are returned to you. It is the law of attraction. What you focus on is what you draw into your life.

I think you'll find that being kind to strangers isn't that difficult. The real challenge is being kind and understanding with those who are closest to us. It's one thing to deal with people out in public, people you don't know; but it's completely different when dealing with difficult family members. Dealing with a negative family member may be the biggest challenge most people face.

It can be especially difficult if you live with someone who is depressed, negative, and unhappy with the course his or her life is taking. But don't let that situation stop you from moving forward with your own life. Please don't let that prevent you from having fun, choosing joy and peace. I get that you may find it especially challenging to stay grounded. It's too easy to match the person's negativity, but you don't need to do that. Focus on your own self-care. There are plenty of self-care options, which we will get into later, but the very best thing you can do for yourself in a moment of stress is to take a deep breath. Break away for just a few minutes and practice mindfulness and meditation, even if it's only for that brief period. Focus on staying centered, breathing in love and out frustration and negativity. When you are grounded and present, you will see that someone's negativity isn't because or about you.

You may not realize this, but is it also not your problem? You don't need to fix the person. You *can't* fix him or her. You have your journey in life, and that person has his or hers. You may see that you're on the journey together, and you are in many ways, but that person's journey is his or her own. You need to allow others the time and space to work out what they need to. I'm not saying not to be supportive; I'm just saying you should stop trying to fix everyone and everything. Their situation is none of your business, and the cost is too high. You know what I'm talking about. If you're a good codependent—always running around and trying to save everyone, fix everyone's problems, and carry the weight of the world—I guarantee you feel like shit, are very unhappy, and feel stressed and overwhelmed.

One of my favorite sayings is "Not my monkeys, not my circus." It may sound cold and uncaring, but sometimes the most loving thing you can do for others is to allow them to do life on their own terms. You can be there and support them but stay in the light, be an example of hope, and mind your own damn business. Allow others the space to learn and grow without getting in the way. Stop putting yourself in the center of everyone else's drama.

I understand you can take care of yourself, doing your best to stay grounded and keeping healthy boundaries, and still struggle with the overwhelming negativity you feel from others. Just stop fighting and taking on their issues; change your focus. Focus your own consciousness.

Let's talk about healthy boundaries for just a minute. It's really important to take a look at this area of your life. When I say "boundaries," I am talking about having healthy connections with others. I'm not talking about building walls to keep people out. I'm saying that you need to consider your needs first. I know what you're thinking. *That's selfish.* I disagree. I think it may be the most loving thing you can do. Establish some guidelines as to what you will and won't allow or do in relationships. Stop worrying about always pleasing others. Stop giving advice, blaming, and accepting blame. Avoid becoming so enmeshed with others that you don't know where you end and they begin.

I remember my professor who taught marriage and family; he explained it like this. She said to picture the letter *A*. If you split the *A* down the middle, neither side could stand alone. Now picture the letter *H*. This time if you separate the letter down the middle, each side can stand alone. You see, the two sides can stand alone but are still connected. You want to be able to stand on your own yet still be connected. The same is true for your loved ones—your children, for example. You want the connection but desire them to be able to stand on their own. You never want others to be so depended on you that they can't do anything for themselves. If it makes you feel better, you can think of the situation this way: you want to empower others, not take their power.

The type of connections you have with others can be critical to your psychological and emotional well-being. By setting healthy boundaries, you will experience less stress and anxiety. You may make some room in your life for joy.

But let's get back to talking about consciousness. It has been said that the quality of your life reflects the quality of your consciousness. We must intentionally raise our level of consciousness to increase the quality of our lives. When I'm talking about consciousness, I'm talking about a state of mind, an increased awareness and connection to the Divine.

Of course, you can raise your level of consciousness by getting still and quiet. I mentioned this before, but it's worth repeating. Meditation has drastically impacted the quality of my life and changed my outlook. It has allowed me to manage my emotions better. It has increased my productivity and creativity. It has allowed me to figure out who I am and establish healthy boundaries with others. For years, I was lost and had no clue who I was. I had lost my identity. I was enmeshed with whomever I was in a relationship with at the time. Others defined my life as I followed the rules they had created for me. Just to be clear, no one ever said, "Here are the rules." But many rules are unspoken and come in the form of expectation. And sometimes these bullshit rules are ones I created for myself to gain love and acceptance, and some I created just to stay safe. I'm sure you know what I'm talking about. We think that for someone to love and accept us, we need to compromise. Sometimes we compromise on little things, such as where to hang the picture, but too often we compromise who we are. If we do this enough times, we totally forget who and what we really are and what we really believe.

I have found that once I slowed down, got quiet, and sat with myself, I was able to figure out who I was, minus the bullshit rules and stories. I was able to get to know the real me once again. I was able to connect with self. Slowing down allowed me access to my inner voice. Once I was able to recognize that still, small voice, I began to experience more synchronicity in my life, and I found I had fewer struggles with more peace and joy. Consider this: if you have friends you believe you are close to but never spend time with them or hear what they have to say, how well do you really know them? If you never spend quiet time with yourself, how can you know who you are?

Chapter 3

Meditation

—⊙§⊙—

Suffering is due to our disconnection with the inner soul.
Meditation is establishing that connection.

—Amit Ray

I know you may be saying, "That is all fine and good, Erica, but how the hell am I supposed to slow down, become vulnerable, and let go of fear and control?" Listen, I'm not saying the process is easy, just that it's possible. You *can* live in this space. This is probably an appropriate time to share with you some of the ways I have made the shift in my life. I have to warn you—if you're looking for a quick fix, this isn't it. This process has taken me several years to figure out. I have had to practice a new way of thinking and being. The reason I've chosen to share all this with you is hopefully to make the journey a little easier for you by laying out some of the shifts I made to come to a place of increased freedom, joy, abundance, and love.

Let's take a closer look at mindfulness and meditation. All meditation is mindfulness, but not all mindfulness is meditation.

Mindfulness

Mindfulness is attention and acceptance without judgment or reaction. Mindfulness keeps us present and grounded. It allows us to stay calm, focused, and clear; and it prevents us from lashing out. Mindfulness keeps us from going into fight or flight. Since we no longer have woolly mammoths chasing us, the fight-or-flight response no longer serves us. Mindfulness is a nonjudgmental response or awareness of thoughts, feelings, and sensations. Mindfulness allows us to pause and observe before responding rather than reacting. Mindfulness allows us to make decisions from a better place. It reminds me of a sign that hung in the classroom of a special education classroom where I taught many years ago. It was a picture of a stop sign, STOP being an acronym for

- Stop,
- Think,
- Consider your options, and
- Perform your action.

So how do we practice mindfulness? By practicing. Meditation is a fantastic way to become more mindful, but here are some practical ways to practice mindfulness:

Suspend Judgment

Stop judging yourself and everyone around you. Things don't need to be categorized as good or bad. Maybe they just are. You need to start by recognizing those judgmental thoughts. Recognize them, then let them move on like a train in the train station or clouds passing by. By observing your thoughts and feelings, you separate yourself from them, because the fact is that you aren't your thought and feelings. You are higher and separate.

Color a Mandala

Mandala is the Sanskrit work for "circle" and represents wholeness and never-ending life. Mandalas have spiritual significance for many religions, often representing the Universe.

The use of a mandala can aid in mindfulness and meditation. By focusing attention, you can achieve a trancelike state. Don't worry, you won't go into some weird trance and hypnotize yourself. But you will relax your mind and make it easier to feel you have moved into a sacred space as well as enhance your spiritual connection. This practice will also help you bring balance your body, your mind, and your spirit and who can't use a little balance. So maybe it's time to slow down, play some relaxing music, and just color.

You can find some cool mandala coloring books these days, and there are plenty of sites that offer free mandala downloads.

Notice Your Breath

I don't mean to check for bad breath and reach for a Tic Tac. I mean to pay attention to how you are breathing. Are you taking short, shallow breaths? If you are, sit up straight and change your breath to deep and full belly breaths. Notice how different that feels. Check out the app called BellyBio Interactive Breathing. It's a pretty cool way to play with your breath and practice deep, controlled breathing. This app offers deep abdominal breathing biofeedback. It teaches how to breathe naturally, deeply, and slowly from your belly.

Mix It Up

One way to be here now is to drive a different way to the grocery store, work, or the gym, even if that means it takes you a little longer to get there. Enjoy the ride. We get so trapped by our routines that we go into autopilot. Take your life off autopilot and actively engage with the world around you. Approach life with a beginner's mind-set. Maybe tonight, before you go to bed, brush your teeth with your opposite hand. Or maybe try to reverse the order in which you do things. Put your socks on before you put on your underwear. Eat something different for breakfast or maybe sit in a different seat at the dinner table. You may be surprised by what you notice when you come from a place of intention as opposed to automation.

Take a Hike

Get outside, put your phone on silent, and listen to the whisper of the wind, the rustle of the trees, the sweet song of the birds serenading you, or the soothing sound of a babbling brook. These sounds calm the brain. A side benefit is that they also reduce blood pressure. If you want to increase the grounding effect of nature, take your shoes off and walk barefoot outside—but not on the concrete. Get in the grass or dirt and feel the earth under your feet.

Take a moment to observe the sights around you. Witness life unfolding. Spiritual leader Thich Nhat Hanh says we should "walk as if [we] are kissing the earth with [our] feet." In other words, notice your feet connecting to Mother Earth. Raise your awareness of your own body—how it moves and supports you. Spending time with nature is a great way to get grounded and feel connected to something larger then you. The Japanese have a practice called "Shinrin-Yoku," which means "forest bathing." They believe spending time in nature has healing power and supports the immune system. There is actually research that supports this idea.

When is the last time you hugged a tree? I bet it has been a while. Hippies shouldn't be the only ones who benefit from the healing power of trees. Did you know there are some real benefits to hugging a tree? Matthew Silverstone explored the unique healing properties of trees in his book *Blinded by Science*. Silverstone scientifically proves the benefits of being exposed to trees. You may already know that each atom vibrates at a different frequency. But did you know trees have a unique vibrational pattern that can have positive biological effects? For example, just being exposed to trees can increase oxytocin levels and release serotonin and dopamine. Those are what I call "feel-good hormones." What that means is that you will experience increased calmness and feel a little happier.

Learn Names

Are you bad with names? When you meet someone new, make a point to learn his or her name. If you aren't listening and aren't present, you will never even hear his or her name. I have been practicing this. I honestly never used to listen when someone introduced himself or herself. Maybe this was because my connections with others was so damaged that I didn't make it important. Most of the time I was distracted and honestly didn't listen. Now I often have to ask people to repeat their names, and then I intentionally use their names as soon as I can. Sometimes I'll just whisper the name to myself so I won't forget.

The side benefit of this practice is that the other person feels important, and it assists with cultivating relationships. Who doesn't like to hear his or her own name? It's more than a feel-good technique. A study that focused on "Brain Activation When Hearing One's Own and Others' Names" by Dennis P. Carmody and Michael Lewis indicates a positive correlation between hearing one's name and brain function and development. It's a win-win. You get to practice mindfulness, other people get the benefit of hearing their names, and you may make them feel important.

Be Intentional

Try to live life from a place of intention. *Choose* happiness and joy. *Choose* to find something to laugh about. Abraham Hicks teaches us to "choose a better feeling thought." You are more in control of your life than you may believe. Small shifts in thinking and actively participating in your life can have dramatic effects on your experience.

Have you ever considered the impact of what you watch and listen to? Choose carefully what you watch on television and pay attention to how certain shows may change the way you feel. I personally choose not to watch the news. I would rather read a newspaper so I can filter what I'm exposed to daily. I choose not to watch violent or scary movies. I don't like how they make me feel. I choose movies that allow me to feel joy and love. You may also want to consider monitoring the time you spend on social media. How do you feel after you have spent an hour mindlessly scrolling through other people's news feeds?

Be intentional with how you use your time. They say people check their phones over 150 times a day. It is estimated that people spend just under two hours a day on social media. It's funny how no one has time to exercise, though. If you think you spend less time on social media than the average person, see whether that is true by downloading one of the many apps that provide you with reports regarding your time spent there. If you really pay attention, you find lots of wasted and unproductive, mindless time during your day. You will find that you can control your day rather than let your day control you. Think of what you could accomplish if you had an extra hour in your day.

Taste Your Food

How many times have you gobbled your food down without even tasting what you're eating? Are you eating while standing up or sitting in the car? Mindful eating allows you to focus intentionally on your food. Notice the taste, texture, temperature, flavors, smells, and colors of your food. Start getting rid of any distractions while you're eating (for example, television or computer), take a deep breath, and notice how you're feeling. Are you satisfied or starting to feel full? As you begin to eat, savor each bite, taste your food, and chew intentionally. Act as if this is the first time you are tasting this dish. Keep in mind that you don't need to judge your food as "good" or "bad." Just enjoy it and bring your awareness back to the food and how it makes you feel.

Did you know that by slowing down when you eat, you are actually helping digestion and nutrient absorption? You will actually help your stomach metabolize your food, which by the way will help you maintain a healthy weight. Start by taking smaller bites. Experts at Ohio State University suggest that you chew softer foods five to ten times and denser foods up to thirty times before swallowing.

Live in the Present

Stop replaying hurts and stories from the past. You don't live there anymore. And quit worrying about tomorrow. The Bible teaches us that tomorrow will take care of itself. Matthew 6:25–27 tells us not to worry about our lives. You don't have to worry about what you will eat or drink. And you don't have to worry about what you will wear. This passage reminds us to look at the birds of the air and notice how God takes care of them. Aren't you more important then the birds? It basically says that if you are more important then the birds that fly, and God takes care of them, then why on earth are you worried?

You've heard people ask the question. If you knew today was going to be your last day on earth, how would you spend it? Make time today to do something that brings you joy. There was a time when I was so lost that I didn't even know what brought me joy. If this is you, take some time to do some pleasure research. Don't start blushing. I'm not just talking about sexual pleasure. I'm talking about anything that brings you pleasure, happiness, joy, excitement, or contentment. If you don't know what makes you feel good, then it's time to start doing some research. Try something new and different, and see how it makes you feel.

Meditation

Now let's talk specifically about meditation, which means "transforming the mind." Practicing meditation doesn't mean you need to become a vegetarian, drink lattes, and do yoga. Practicing meditation is all about slowing down and taking control over your own state of mind and well-being. It's about increasing your awareness and ability to be present. It allows you to be free from the circus or "monkey brain" as many sages have called it. Buddhists call it a "monkey mind," meaning unsettled, restless, and uncontrollable. Meditation means sitting quietly and listening to one's body and breath, not the crazy chatter in your head.

If you're tired of the crazy, rushing thoughts that keep you up at night and reaching for something to help you fall asleep, then you may want to consider the following benefits of meditation:

- It reduces stress and anxiety.
- It improves the quality of your life and relationships as you experience an increased feeling of connection.
- It slows the aging process. How nice is that?
- It may improve your ability to concentrate.

- Your doctor will be happy, since meditation reduces blood pressure and improves cardiovascular and immune health.
- And oh yes—meditation improves sleep.

Before I get into my own meditation practice, let's talk about some of the more popular forms of meditation:

Zen: This type of meditation involves counting the breath to quiet the mind. It shifts the focus from your monkey brain to your breathing.

Vipassana Meditation: Here the focus is on your own body, noticing any sensations to develop insight into the nature of self and reality. It shifts attention from your thoughts to your body. The term means "to see things as they really are."

Loving-Kindness: This type of meditation helps to develop positive feelings toward self and others. You do this by first offering love to yourself, then to your loved one and moving out to people with whom you may be in conflict. That's right, you offer love and a higher vibration even to people who don't elicit a positive feeling from you. From there, you send love to your community, then move out to the world. You will find that as you practice this, you increase the love you feel for others, even those people who challenge you.

Mantra: This is a chanting meditation during which a word or sound is repeated. One common mantra is *om*. Here again we shift focus from our thoughts to something greater than us. *Om* isn't necessarily a word; it is a symbol (ॐ) that is considered "the sound of the universe." It represents all that is. It is the oneness of all creation, including the heavens and earth. *Om*, when said, sounds like A-U-M. Check out the benefits of chanting *om*.

- Chanting of the *om* a creates a positive vibration in you, making you feel happier. It is said to purify your aura.
- Chanting *om* gives a vibration felt through your vocal cords that benefits your sinuses and thyroid glands.

- Om chanting actually improves your voice by giving strength to your vocal cords.
- When generating the sound from your abdomen, you strengthen your spinal cord by strengthening the supporting muscles.

Transcendental Meditation (TM): This type of meditation seems popular with some pretty famous people, including Oprah Winfrey and the Beatles. Maharishi Mahesh Yogi introduced this technique in India in the 1950s. This type of meditation is practiced for twenty minutes a day to induce a sense of deep rest and calm within the body and brain.

Chakra Meditation: This one may seem a little more confusing because this meditation focuses on the seven chakras. *Chakra* is a Sanskrit word that means "wheel or spinning disc." Each chakra represents various energy points on the body that align with the spine. You want the chakras to be open, meaning you want the energy moving and going in the right direction.

To practice this meditation, breathe deeply and focus on your breath moving all the way down to the base of your spine. And then notice the breath moving back up on the inhalation. After a few deep breaths, focus your attention on each chakra. Visualize the chakra being open, spinning to the right, and sense the energy in each chakra growing stronger. Let's take a minute to take a closer look at each chakra

> First Chakra, Root Chakra: This chakra can be found at the base of the spine and is represented by the color red. The first chakra is responsible for stability, security, and our basic needs. When the energy of this chakra is open and flowing in the right direction, we feel safe and fearless.
>
> Second Chakra: The sacral chakra can be found just above the pubic bone and below the belly

button. This, our creativity and sexual center, is responsible for our creative expression. This chakra is represented by the color orange.

Third Chakra: The solar plexus chakra is represented by the color yellow and can be found just below the breastbone but above the belly button. The third chakra is our source of personal power and is what keeps us moving forward.

Fourth Chakra: This powerful chakra is the heart chakra, located at your heart center and represented by the color green. The heart chakra serves as a bridge between our bodies, minds, emotions, and spirits. The heart chakra is our source of love and connection.

Fifth Chakra: The throat chakra is located in the area of the throat. This is our source of verbal expression and the ability to speak our highest truth; it is represented by the color blue.

Sixth Chakra: Also referred to as the Third Eye and represented by the color indigo, this chakra is located between the eyebrows. This is the center of intuition. Focus on opening the sixth chakra; this will help increase your intuition.

Seventh Chakra: The crown chakra is located at the very top of your head, your crown. This is the chakra of enlightenment and spiritual connection to our higher selves, ultimately to the Divine. The crown chakra is represented by the color violet.

Contemplative Prayer: This type of meditation originates from the Christian tradition and is similar to the mantra meditation, in that it involves focusing on one word over and over as a way to clear the mind. Thomas Merton, a Catholic theologian, mystic, and writer, taught this mode of meditation.

Brace yourself. This next one is going to sound out there, but knowledge is power, so here we go.

OM: OM is orgasmic meditation. OneTaste NYC is leading the way in making orgasmic meditation known. They offer a safe space for practitioners, classes and OM coaching. OneTaste describes OM as a "consciousness practice you do with another person. During OM, one person strokes another person's clitoris for 15 minutes with no goal other than to feel sensation. The OM practice combines the power and attention of meditation with the deeply human, deeply felt, and connected experience of orgasm." One Taste has taken the lead on this type of meditation. They say "orgasm magnifies, intensifies, and vivifies everyday experience not altering it, but by revealing its true nature. The implications for our health, happiness, and relationships are astounding."

Now that we got that out of the way, I can share with you what I do, and that is whatever the hell I feel like doing. Sometimes I make it up as I go. I used to look for clear instructions on how to meditate. I have since come to realize that meditation is very personal and can be as unique as the individual. There is something freeing about having this time and space to create whatever I want. Don't burn me at the stake for saying this, but it's like creating your own personal religion. There are no rules; it's about what feels good or right to you. Meditation is a personal journey and experience.

It is fun and helpful to have a specific spot in your house or office to use for meditation, but you sure don't have to. I have a friend who converted her kids' treehouse into a cute little meditation/yoga space. She even installed a small wood-burning stove to keep it cozy on those frigid winter days. You don't have to get that elaborate. I had another friend who created a mini-altar in her closet.

I enjoyed the freedom to take what I have learned from various sources and religions to create something that meets my needs. I like to pull out all the good stuff and leave what doesn't serve me. I like having no rules when it comes to my spirituality or meditation practice. I like creating my own ritual. Remember, I grew up going to Catholic schools; I needed to know when to sit, stand, and kneel. I had to memorize what I was supposed to say and when to say it. It doesn't get more rigid and ceremonial than that. It has taken me a long time to shed the rules of religion, which kept me believing there was only one way to connect with God. I'm not saying you need to change religions or anything like that. I'm just saying your spiritual journey is very personal. Think independently and search for what feels right to you. I do want to point out that if you do your research, you will find that most, if not all, religions support the idea of meditation. Hindu, Buddhist, Taoist, Jewish, Christian, and Islamic traditions all support the idea of meditation. Psalm 104:34 references a desire for our meditation to be pleasing to God.

In all honesty, I feel more connected to the Divine, myself, and others now than at any other point in my life. I believe my meditation practice has changed the course of my life. I begin my meditation with my own ritual, which that goes like this:

- There is a zafu or meditation pillow in front of my altar.* I find that it's more comfortable than sitting on the floor, and it keeps me sitting up straight and not all slouched. Sometimes I lie down on a yoga mat, but I feel like sitting up allows me to be more intentional, and I'm not likely to fall asleep while doing so. When I have time, I lie down. It's okay to fall asleep while you're meditating. If you fall asleep, that's because your body needs it.
- Once I get situated, I turn on my favorite song for meditation, "Devi Prayer" by Craig Puess and Ananda. I also like Wayne Dyer's "Wishes Fulfilled Meditation." I have used guided meditations in the past. These are great when you're first getting started, and they are a wonderful way to get ideas.

While lighting the candles, I repeat the Invocation to "Light" by Tashira Tashi-ren.

I live within the light
I love within the light
I laugh within the light
I am sustained and nourished by the light
I joyously serve the light
For, I am light, I AM light, I am Light
I am that I am, in all that I do

- Next, I take a few deep breaths to get grounded.
- I have a deck of Angel Cards by Doreen Virtue, which I keep at my altar. I will grab the cards, pray for guidance and direction, and flip a card. Before picking a card, I pray this little prayer I found in Tosha Silver's book *Outrageous Openness*: "Open me, Divine to all that I need to know, and allow me to be open to the changes that you wish for me."
- I mentioned that I keep various crystals on my altar; I think there are ten of them. Sometimes I pick up each crystal, one at a time, hold it in my hand, and name something I am grateful for before putting it back in place. It is believed that various crystals have healing properties. Each crystal holds a different energy. For example, rose quartz is used to increase unconditional love.
- Sometimes I set a timer if I'm limited on time and want to make sure I don't take too long, or I will set it if I want to sit for a specific period. Most of the time I don't set the timer; I just meditate until I feel like I'm done.
- I have tried different approaches.
  - Sometimes I like to count my breaths. I do this by touching my pointer finger and thumb on the first breath, my thumb and middle finger on the next, and so on. I may do this for a few rounds just to get started.
  - Other times I focus my attention on the sensations in my body. Feeling my feet touching the floor, my ass on

the cushion, my legs, and abdomen, I work my way up my spine and to the top of my head, noticing how each section of my body feels.

- There are times when I will choose to focus my attention on each chakra or give myself Reiki. I am a Reiki level-one practitioner. For those unfamiliar with Reiki, it is a Japanese healing technique that uses the movement of energy in the body. The word *Reiki* is made up from two Japanese words—*Rei* means "God's Wisdom or the Higher Power," and *Ki* means "life force energy." So Reiki is actually "spiritually guided life force energy" that is moving through your body. It is based on the idea that an unseen "life force energy" flows through us.

- On days I'm struggling with emotion, I imagine myself breathing in love and exhaling feelings that don't serve me. It's a way of letting go and visualizing the negativity leaving my body. I also like to do a loving-kindness meditation, sending love to those with whom I am in conflict.

If you have strong religious beliefs, you can create a meditation that stays true to your beliefs and who you are. For example, praying the rosary is a great meditation. It doesn't have to be weird—woo woo—or out of alignment with what you believe. You just need it to be right for you. The important part is that you take the time to quiet your mind.

Chapter 4

From Fear to Follow

Fear defeats more people than any other one thing in the world.

—Ralph Waldo Emerson

Overcontrolling our lives is one way many of us deal with fear. We try to control everything we touch—everyone in our lives and just about anything that may rock the boat. We try to keep things consistent and try to avoid the unexpected. When we do this, we leave little room for the divine inspiration. My need for control kept me obsessing over the future, and I worried about what might happen. I was so consumed with fear and anxiety that I was missing the beauty in the moment. "Doing" was more important to me than "being." Fighting for control conflicts with having fun. I may be a living testament to this truth. I spent too many years void of joy, fun, and laughter.

My friend, a gay pastor from South Carolina, used to say in his very southern accent, "Girl, God knows, God cares, and he's already worked it out. So, stop worrying."

I would try to say, "But Jason—"

And he would cut me off before I could explain why I needed

to worry, and he would just say, "Already." Jason was right; there is no need to worry. God has already worked it out on your behalf.

Some say worry is like praying for what you don't want. I used to worry about everything, and I do mean *everything*. Living in fear, I was always hypervigilant, looking to detect anything that may cause me harm. My way of managing worry was to manage everything about my life. I tried to avoid surprises, anticipate letdowns, and predict disappointments. I was always on the offense, ready to duck and weave. All my attempts to control my life were pointless. They just made me feel more out of control, worried, and stressed. The funny thing is that the worrying I did never did a lick of good. It never helped change the outcome of anything. Now I know that being stressed and worried about what could possibly go wrong is a total waste of time and energy. It has never made anything in my life better. The only difference it made in my life was to intensify my negative feelings and make my view of the situation seem worse than it actually was. If anything was going well, it wasn't likely that I would have noticed. I was too busy worrying. When I did notice things were going well, my worry and anxiety increased. I figured they couldn't stay good for long; something bad was bound to happen. Do you see the problem?

I also used to be very reactive, ready for the catastrophic. You could say, "Erica, I need to talk to you," and I would go right to assuming the worst. Straight to panic. Once I learned to "slow the fuck down," I was able to take a deep breath and wait to get all the information and consider my options instead of curling up in a ball and crying in the corner like a baby. For example, I was having computer problems last week, so I went to spend some quality time with the Apple genius guys (sarcasm) who said we would have to do a backup of the computer, wipe it clean, and then restore everything. They did their best to assure me that everything would be saved; of course, I was nervous; I had years of work saved on that computer. After I got my computer back, I got to work on the finishing touches of this book. The only problem was that when I opened the document, everything was gone. There were only two paragraphs. I started breathing heavily, and I felt panic starting to creep in. I have to remind myself of the old saying "Cooler heads prevail," and I committed to trying everything before crying. After taking a deep breath—voilà —everything was there. It was just that some little box had been checked that shouldn't have been.

I have had to give up on the idea of controlling and protecting my life. When you are present and can learn just to be, life is less stressful. Looking back, I can see that all those times when I tried to control my life and the lives of others, the more out of control I felt. The more I tried to avoid feeling rejection, disappointment, and inadequacy, the more I felt all those things. We often hold so tightly to everything in our lives when all we are looking for can be found when we release control of people and situations. Unclench your teeth and your fist, and relax.

The opposite of control is vulnerability, a willingness to let go. Maybe you have experienced the fear of being in a new relationship, fearful it won't work out and that you'll get hurt. That fear prevents you from enjoying the moment. It puts you on guard, on the defense. Move beyond fear and give that relationship a chance; even if it doesn't work out, I bet you will learn some important lessons about yourself. Our connection with others begins when we shift from control to vulnerability.

Motivational speaker, author, and social worker Brene' Brown may have said it best: "I spent a lot of years trying to outrun or outsmart vulnerability by making things certain and definite, black and white, good and bad. My inability to lean into the discomfort of vulnerability limited the fullness of those important experiences that are wrought with uncertainty: Love, belonging, trust, joy, and creativity to name a few."

I once took a bike ride with my daughter. The plan was to ride our bikes on a trail that runs along the Delaware River from Washington Crossing, Pennsylvania, up to New Hope, Pennsylvania, a trip we had made before. It's only the next town over and about a fifteen-minute car ride. So off we went, and a few minutes into the bike ride, I realized my bike's odometer wasn't working, so I had no idea how far we had gone, which meant I had no idea how much farther we would need to go. I had no idea where we were on our little journey. I became obsessed with wanting to know how much farther we had to go to reach our destination. I was so consumed and distracted with this missing information that I didn't enjoy the journey.

The same has been true for most of my life. I am on a path, I know I will make it, I know I have gone through this before, I know I am safe, yet I am so caught up in the process and getting to the destination that I miss the great stuff along the way. It's a much different experience when I relax and enjoy the journey, unworried about the details of the trip. It's a much more pleasant experience when I can just be—be present, be content, be myself. Just be in the moment and not worry about the details. But it's my need for some false sense of control that always seems to get me tripped up. I'm learning that I can't control situations; I can control only how I react to them. I had to start learning to control my inside rather than my outside. So let me ask (insert dramatic pause), Do you waste energy trying to create, push, or force life? Are you trying to make life happen according to your timeline? Do you freak out if you don't have every little detail figured out?

Or do you have faith that God is in control and that Divine timing is perfect? And don't try to tell me that you have a little faith. You can't. It's impossible. It is like being a little pregnant; either you are pregnant, or you aren't. You can't be a little pregnant, and you can't have a little bit of faith. When I say, "Just be," that takes complete faith. Complete release. Complete vulnerability. Complete surrender to something bigger than ourselves.

We have all experienced fear. Fear is our innate reaction designed to keep us safe, but too often it is fear that prevents us from playing full out. Fear prevents us from living the life of our dreams. Fear is what keeps us silent when we should speak. It keeps us still when we should move. Fear keeps us in relationships too long, and it keeps us locked in jobs we hate. Fear prevents us from taking chances and moving forward.

How can we take our lives to the next level if we have a fear of love, fear of money, fear of power, fear of loss, fear of poverty, fear of pain, fear of letting go? We can't. How many opportunities have you missed because of fear? How has holding tight to a piece of your life ever served you? I played small for many years, but I refuse to live as a hostage to fear any longer.

Fear is an ugly crippling thing. People who know me now might be surprised to hear this, but I spent most of my life afraid—afraid of trying, feeling, speaking up, and failing. Afraid of not being good or smart enough. Even afraid of being in a situation where I wouldn't know what to do or say. I declined invitations to events if I didn't know how to get there or even where to park. I shied away from parties for fear that I wouldn't have anyone to talk to; or worse yet, someone would talk to me, and I wouldn't know what to say. I was afraid I would get tongue tied and sound like an idiot. Don't believe me? I remember when I was fifteen. I had a bunch of new friends over to my house, and there were even a few boys in the bunch. I was so nervous and totally out of my comfort zone. I remember telling some goofy story about an octopus, and I meant to say *tentacles*, but I said *testicles* instead. Everyone died laughing, but it took me a minute to catch on, and when I did, I was mortified. Their laughter rang in my ears for years. After that, the scared part of me always whispered, "Keep your mouth shut and don't say anything so that you don't sound like a fool."

My fear of life was so bad that I was afraid to go to the mailbox, afraid to find an unexpected bill I couldn't pay. I was afraid to face my financial situation.

Today I don't fear, fear. Remember the Disney movie *Monsters, Inc.*? If you saw the movie, you may remember that the children were afraid to open the closet doors in their bedrooms. They were terrified of the monsters they thought were hiding there and under their beds. But one child, named Boo, had the courage to open the closet door; and what she found wasn't so scary. Yes, there were monsters in the closet (and one of them was kind of ugly), but they weren't at all scary. One was big and goofy, and the other was a little one-eyed monster who was more afraid of Boo then she was of him.

I have found that life is much like the movie. Fear of monsters can keep us up at night, hiding under our covers, afraid of strange sounds, afraid to open the door. But sometimes, if we can gather enough courage to open the closet door of our lives, what we find inside isn't so scary. It may be an ugly, one-eyed mess, but it's usually not as bad as we expect.

What might happen if you took a deep breath and faced that one thing that keeps you up at night? What I now know for sure is that there is freedom on the other side of fear.

My birthday and Mother's Day are the two days of the year when I know my kids will do just about anything I ask them to do. So on my last birthday, I rounded up the troops (my husband Michael, Danny, Gabriella, and Selina) and headed to the local indoor rock-climbing gym. We all put on the funky shoes and prepared for our brief lesson on how to climb. We walked in, slipped on the harness, and hooked up at the auto belay. Rather than having to count on someone to hold the rope and make sure you get down safely, they hook beginners up to the auto belay. This is sort of a pulley system that slowly lowers you to the ground when you come off the wall. It's like an automatic braking system so you don't splatter on the floor if you fall.

Before even touching the wall, I looked up and planned my route to the top. I grabbed the wall fully, intent on making it to the top on my first try. I started climbing, got about four feet off the ground, and froze. I was overcome with fear. All I could think about was falling off the wall. Hands sweating, I slowly climbed my way back down. I hung back and watched my family try to climb before I tried again. After several attempts, I inched higher than last time, but I was still climbing down rather than relying on the belay to help me get down.

One of the workers came over to me and said, "You're not supposed to climb down. Just let go of the wall, and let the belay lower you." Now everyone was watching, and I was supposed to trust the belay to prevent me from becoming one with the floor. I climbed four feet and promised to try to let go and trust the belay. When I finally let go of the wall, I felt a sudden, quick little drop (I experienced immediate panic) before the belay kicked in. Because I freaked out, I spun around and skidded down the bumps on the wall, landing flat on my back. Not a very graceful descent. My daughter walked up, stood over me as I lay there, sprawled out on the floor, and told me I looked like a starfish that had washed up on the beach. I lay there, thinking, *This guy is crazy if he thinks for one second that I am going to let go of the wall from all the way up there*, which was about forty feet.

Letting go of the wall and trusting the belay were really a challenge. I realized that if I stood a chance of making it to the top, I was going to need to practice falling and remind myself that I wasn't going to get hurt. There was enough evidence that I wouldn't get hurt. Everyone around me was using the belay, and everyone landed on his or her feet uninjured. After I mastered falling from a few feet, I was able to climb higher until I was able to successfully climb to the top. Learning to fall and fail is critical to any progress. I experienced something similar way back when I was learning yoga. We were practicing one of those fancy balance moves, called "crow pose"; my knees were on my elbows, and I was balancing all my weight on my hands. I remember the instructor telling us that it was okay to fall—that once we fell, we would find the edge of our balance and know how far we could go.

Failure once terrified me. I was stuck in my own head. I would rather not try than to try and fail. Because of this, as a kid I was the worst student ever. As a high school guidance counselor, I used to tell kids it was a wonder that I ever graduated from high school, and it was a miracle that I went to college. Today the fact is mind blowing that I graduated from Clemson University, and I have a master's degree from the University of South Florida. Who would have ever believed that I would consider pursuing a doctorate? I literally laugh to myself. Prior to graduating from high school, I refused to try. In my head, I knew I was stupid, but I didn't want everyone else to know just how stupid I was. So for me it was easier to say that I failed because I didn't try. But the truth was that I didn't try because I was convinced that I would fail anyway. I knew that if I tried and still failed, I would prove I was as dumb as I thought I was.

At some point after the age of eighteen, I learned how I learned. I figured out how to study and get decent grades. Better yet, I began to love learning. But as an adult, my fear crippled me in other ways. Fear dictated my life. Fear won out over love. Fear was the driving force in every relationship; it affected my finances and robbed me of joy, fun, and pleasure.

If you are looking to live your life full out, you're going to have to drop the resistance, trust in something greater than yourself, and release the fear. The only way I know to do this is by calming the mind and quieting that voice in my head. In Dan Harris's book, *10% Happier*, he talks about that voice in his own head; and he says, "The voice in my head is an asshole." I'm with you, Dan. The voice in my head is the same.

Chapter 5

Relationships

⸻ ❧ ⸻

No one saves us but ourselves. No one can, and no
one may. We ourselves must walk the path.

—Buddha

At the age of twenty-one, I got married. I didn't realize it at the time, but looking back, I believe I got married not because I loved him but because I thought I was supposed to marry him. We had been dating since I was eighteen, and marriage seemed to be the next step. I was also afraid he was my only option. I was afraid of what would happen if I said no, if I broke things off, or if I was alone. No lie, the day we married was the day I knew I had made a horrible mistake. It was fear that kept me in that marriage. I was so afraid of the unknown that I was stuck. If I asked for a divorce, what would happen to the kids? Where would I live? How would I support myself and my girls? What would happen to me? What would other people say? I had never really been on my own. How on earth could I survive?

I was miserable, and looking back, I was incredibly mean to my ex-husband. I hated him. And I do mean hate. I believed he had ruined my life. I was so resentful and angry; I couldn't give two shits about him. It was eleven years of hatred and anger stacked up year upon year. But nobody knew. I never told anyone how I felt or why I was so vicious. I never allowed myself to be vulnerable enough with anyone to share my pain. I was so afraid of being judged that I just let the anger boil within me, and it showed. I walked around with arms crossed, lips pursed, and eyebrows pinched. I am sure you know the look, and you know it isn't a good look for anyone. Looking back, I see how ugly I was. I mean, I had a really ugly spirit. I thought I had valid reasons to be angry; things happened in our relationship that no one knew about. The old me used the "story" of what had happened to justify my behavior. I know my story was just that, a story. We all tell ourselves stories about our lives—stories about why we can't have what we want and why things aren't going right for us. Why we haven't accomplished our dreams. And why we can't have our hearts' desires.

What I have learned is that it doesn't matter what your story is. It doesn't matter who hurt you. It doesn't matter what the circumstances are that led to your pain. What matters is what you are going to do with all this. I sat with my story, and my story grew stronger, and so did my anger. But now I know I have options, and so do you. Are you going to allow your situation to cause you to be a victim, or will you allow it to make you stronger? You can be a victim or a victor. If you're going to choose to allow this to make you stronger, then you're going to have to move past fear and let go of the story.

A few weeks ago, a new friend said, "Erica, what's your story?" I knew what she was asking me. She wanted to know more about me; she wanted to know what I had been through in life. All I could tell her was, "I don't have a story. I used to have a story but not anymore. I don't live there. I don't live in the past." I can tell you about who I am today. I have moved to the other side of fear and dropped the limiting beliefs that held me back for so long. In this place, I respect my past, honor my present, and am totally excited for the future. The unknown doesn't cripple me; I now look at the uncertainty of life as an exciting adventure. Instead of saying, "Oh, now what's going to happen to me?" I now think, *I can't wait to see what remarkable thing is around the corner.*

As a school counselor, I encouraged kids to talk about their feelings. I gave the analogy of a trash can. You can shove only so much in there before it all begins to spill on the floor and things begin to get messy. My trash-worthy feelings were beginning to spill all over my life. I didn't know how to deal with my feelings. I didn't know how to take my own trash out, and I sure didn't know how to overcome fear.

What I know today is that fear is overcome with baby steps. You've seen the memes that say, "Do something today that scares you." You overcome fear by taking a deep breath and a small risk. But that is only part of it. I know today that you also overcome fear with faith and gratitude. Remember, fear and faith cannot coexist. But you have to pick one. My life started changing when I chose to cling to faith rather than to fear.

Once out of my first marriage, I wasn't in the clear when it came to relationships. I still had a lot of work to do. I struggled with friendships as well as intimate relationships. It was hard for me to make friends. I'm talking about true friends, not just acquaintances or people to hang out with. I was afraid of being hurt, betrayed, and left. What I was most afraid of was rejection. The hurts of my first marriage left me feeling full of rejection; it became my norm, my model for life and all relationships. I was always afraid that I would be abandoned.

Unless others reached out to me, I kept to myself. I never invited anyone to do anything or go anywhere. I was already convinced they wouldn't want to hang out with me, even before I asked them. If I saw someone in the store I knew, I went down a different aisle and hid. I was afraid to say hello, afraid that they wouldn't even remember me. This is something I have had to consciously work on. I stopped hiding. I started trying to connect. I started taking small risks. Today if I meet others I can easily ask them if they would like to meet again for coffee, something I never, ever would have tried before. My head would have stopped me with, *What if they don't really like me? What if they say no? What if I actually get to know them and have to let them in—and what if once they get to know me, they will see what a loser I am?* I was so afraid of being seen, of being known. I hid in the shadows where I thought I would be safer.

On the flip side of that, if someone asked me to do something (unless it was going to a party), I always said yes. I was starved for attention and craved validation. My need for attention and validation got me into trouble in my intimate relationships. Time after time, someone would pay a little attention to me, and next thing I knew, we were in relationship. I settled for what was in front of me. I felt like I couldn't do better. I always felt like this was my last chance, the last time someone would be interested in me. Even if the relationship sucked and I believed that things couldn't be better, I figured that having someone, even the wrong someone, was better than being alone. My friend's grandmother had a saying when it came to relationships. "Don't bother breaking up with him. You'll just be trading one bag of shit for another." We would follow that up with, "Well, I guess we need to decide which one smells worse." That is such an awful way to look at relationships, but I believed this to be true. It seemed to be my reality.

It's funny. I hear women say all the good ones were taken, but back then I didn't even think there were any good ones, just bad and worse. And for your information, all the good ones aren't taken. Once I pulled my head out of my ass, chose myself over him, and got out of a bad relationship I had no business being in to begin with, things began to turn around. The last relationship I was in before I met my husband was no picnic. But I had settled for so long that I felt trapped. I left like I was on a raft on a raging river, and there was no way off. But with a little self-work (okay, a lot of self-work), I set myself free. It was a whole new world; I was free to figure out who I was as a person. Once I did this, I was able to learn how to relate to others in more meaningful ways. I have to give a shout-out to my therapist for helping me through the end of the relationship and my amazing life coach, who helped put the pieces of my life back together and helped me find myself.

Getting out of this relationship was a practice in mastering stillness in motion. I was working with a therapist who kept telling me to sit still and not react. She asked me to wait to break up with him. She told me to feel, and when the time was right, I could end the relationship. She knew I liked to run and hide from feelings. Because running and hiding were a way of life for me, I had a tough time understanding why she wanted me to wait. But I trusted her, so I did what she suggested. I resisted my urge to impulsively and abruptly end things. I wanted to rip off the Band-Aid and let the pieces fall where they may. What I learned was how to get clarity, how to get silent, how to deal with my feelings, and how to "slow the fuck down." What I learned was that God's timing is perfect.

None of us like to feel. I used to run from my feelings. But guess what? Feelings are just feelings. They won't kill you. It's okay to feel the feelings; just don't attach yourself to them. What I mean is, feel what you need to feel; then let it go.

During those months when I was "mastering stillness in motion," sitting with my emotions and not reacting, waiting for breakup day, I focused on working on me. I focused on my happiness. I focused on getting to know myself again and figuring out who I was outside of the relationship. I worked to add more tools to my toolbox. I also gathered my tribe and focused on neglected friendships. I surrounded myself with others who would support me. I started flexing and strengthening my self-empowerment muscles.

One thing I can tell you without a doubt is that when it came time to break up, I didn't waver. I stood strong and confident. I had a clarity I had never had before. I was clear on what I was willing to put up with and accept in a relationship. I was clear on who I was, what I wanted, and most importantly, what I needed. The old me would have second-guessed my decision, and I would have been easily manipulated into staying in a sick relationship. I would have convinced myself that I couldn't do better than what I had. I believed that I didn't deserve anything better. I assumed this was as good as it was going to get.

Can you stay in a moment, even if it makes you uncomfortable? Do you allow things to flow naturally, or are you always forcing life? Now, I just need to be clear about one thing: in no way am I saying that you should stay longer in a relationship than you should, especially if the relationship is abusive. I'm just saying, "Slow the fuck down." Feel what you need to feel and know that you never again need to react and be impulsive.

One of the most impactful exercises any coach ever had me do was to date myself. For a whole month, I was to date myself and no one else. It was the month of March, my birthday month, and it also happened to be four months before I met my husband. I thought the idea of dating myself was weird. I asked my coach, "How do I do this?" She told me to treat myself like I would want to be treated. I was to treat myself like I would treat someone in a relationship. I was to treat myself like I actually wanted to be treated. She told me to take myself out for dinner and to buy myself flowers—those kinds of things.

During the first few days of my relationship with myself, I realized I would do things for others that I wouldn't go out of the way to do for myself. For example, I was hungry but didn't want to cook something. I had to stop myself. I knew that if someone else had said he or she was hungry, I would have cooked the person something. Somehow, I had the idea that something wasn't worth the hassle if it was just for me. I began to notice that I always felt like I wasn't "worth it."

So this was the beginning of me treating myself with respect and kindness. That year I had the best birthday ever. I took myself shopping, bought myself roses, and called a few friends and asked them to meet me for lunch at my favorite restaurant. I had dinner with my dad, and then later that evening I had a friend come over. We made vision boards and listened to music. It really was the best birthday I ever had. There was no expectation, no waiting for someone else to come along and create a great birthday for me; I created my own experience. My friend Lindsay recently threw herself a big birthday bash with the most beautiful birthday cake. We danced, laughed, and had a great time.* Stop waiting for others to celebrate you. Start living and enjoying your life. Start celebrating.

This past summer my husband bought a business in Cape May, New Jersey, which happens to be two and a half hours from our house. To get the business off the ground, he had to be down on the shore all summer—which meant that if I wanted to see him, I had to go to the shore every weekend. This new arrangement was challenging for me. I had to adjust to a new norm. As I tried to figure out how to balance life, a couple of things suffered, one of which was my house plants. So today as I gave my plants a little extra attention, I noticed there were a lot of dead leaves. As I pruned the plants, I was reminded of how we must prune relationships from time to time. Sometimes we need to cut off the dead spot, and sometimes we are called on to remove a few leaves.

One of my plants was completely dead. I had a choice to make. I could either leave my dead plant sitting right where it was in my kitchen for everyone to see, or I could throw it out and make room for a new plant. As a child, I remember learning that you needed to remove dead leaves, or the plant would waste all its energy on the dead areas rather than using its energy to grow and thrive. Pruning is necessary to make room for new growth. Pruning relationships is the same way. I have learned that pruning or removing relationships that are dead or don't serve my higher good make way for the amazing friends I have in my life today. I am very particular of whom I let in my inner circle. I will help anyone, but people who are unhealthy, negative, or living with low energy don't need to be in my inner circle. What I mean is that I don't spend a lot of time with them, and I don't seek them out.

While we are talking about relationships, I need to speak to the ladies for a minute. If you are a guy, you can skip my mini rant. Okay, girls, what the hell are you doing? I hear how you talk about men. And I have to tell you—they aren't the enemy. I read a crazy Facebook post that went something like this: "Women seem hardened as a result of years of bullshit; as a result they have become cold and void of love. To balance it out men need to take a knee and come and correct." I saw this, and my reaction was something like this: "What the fuck is wrong with women? Why do we blame men for all that is wrong in our lives and in our relationships?"

At what point did we lose ourselves and our power? We have given our power to people who don't deserve it. We have turned over control of our own happiness and joy, and that's fucked up. You aren't a victim, and no one needs to take a knee and correct anything for you. Correct it yourself. Choose joy. Choose love. Start by loving yourself, and you will draw love to you. Stop fearing being hurt in a relationship. You are only drawing in more hurt. When you find joy within, no one can steal that from you. Choose to be warm and loving. Practice with strangers. Practice kindness. Practice being nice. I would bet money that you will find that kindness and love will find you. When you have love, when you give love, you get more of it in return. You will find a man who will drop to his knees for you because he wants to, not because he has to right the wrongs of all those who came before him. Because you are deserving of love and being worshipped, you must see it in yourself first. You need to take ownership of your own shit and stop blaming others. It isn't about them; it's about you. You are responsible for your own happiness. No one is responsible for your happiness but you.

And while we're talking about owning your own shit, stop telling men what's wrong with them and that they need to fix or change everything in their lives. Just stop already. Fix your shit and let him figure out his. When you constantly berate your man, telling them all he did wrong and all he needs to do, you emasculate him. Stop thinking you can get someone else to change. First off, no one needs to change who he is for you, just like you don't need to change who you are for someone else. You may think you want a man who will do whatever you tell him to do, but you really don't. What you will end up with is a man boy who doesn't know who he is and can't stand in his own power. You will have a man whom you have zero respect for. Stop stealing his power; you have your own. Before I end my rant, I will give you an example of what I'm talking about.

I have a friend who has a really great boyfriend. He loves her and would do anything for her—and he does. He worships her and wants to spend his life with her, but last winter he was struggling with depression and didn't tell her what was going on. She was mad that he didn't tell her. Now all my friend talks about is what *he* needs to do to fix his life. Not only does she tell me what he needs to do, but she tells him. Constantly! He needs to see a counselor. He needs to take meds. He needs to be more present. He needs to stop drinking. He needs to be gluten free. He needs to exercise. He needs to make friends. She even tells him what he should order when we go out to eat. She tries to control him, but she is missing all the wonderful things he does for her. In the process, she emasculates him. He is a big boy. He knows what he needs and what he doesn't. He knows how to order off a menu.

The thing is, the situation isn't really about him. It all has to do with her and her need to feel safe. You see how fear can rear its ugly head in relationships? So, what I'm telling you is to focus on you. Stop trying to change and fix those you love. Give them space to figure out their lives. Get grounded so you can find peace.

Chapter 6

Feminine Energy

—ⓢ—

Water is the softest thing, yet, it can penetrate
mountains and earth. This shows clearly the
principle of softness overcoming hardness.

—Lao Zi

I once lived guarded, untouchable, and hardened. This state showed on my face, in the way I carried myself, and in how I interacted with others. I was in control; I was the one making all the decisions. I was stiff and rigid. What I learned is that I embodied a very masculine energy. When I started this journey, I had no idea what living in my feminine energy meant. I was at a Tony Robbins event, where he asked all the women to stand up in their feminine energy. Next, they played a slow, beautiful song and asked us to dance in a way that was slow and flowing. The women around me looked comfortable and sensual. I looked like the Tin Man needing to be greased. I was so uncomfortable, but I came to realize how out of touch I was with my own body and my true nature.

As a society we have a complete misunderstanding of what embracing feminine energy means. Unfortunately, too many women believe, like I once did, that feminine energy is inferior to masculine energy, that it means being weak and taken advantage of by others. People think it means being subservient or being a doormat, but that is far from the truth. Feminine and masculine energies are forces found in each of us. And we all need both energies—one isn't superior to the other, and the two aren't mutually exclusive.

Feminine energy is about being, allowing, accepting, and receiving. Masculine energy is more about doing, striving, pushing forward, and giving. Feminine energy is more passive, agreeable, and accommodating, while masculine energy is active and seeing control. Here is where things get interesting. I know that for many women, the description of feminine energy doesn't sound enticing. *Allowing* and *accepting* aren't bad words. We have been so ingrained with this idea that we have to be tough and strong *all the time*. But that just isn't true. Like I said, we all possess both masculine and feminine energies, and we use both. When I'm at work, I tend to stay more in the masculine energy, because I'm actually in charge and have to get things done. But I don't stay there all the time anymore. I now know how to flow between the two energies, while in the past I lived every moment of my life in the masculine, fighting for control.

And just think about this for a second: what man (one who lives in his masculine energy) wants to compete with the woman in his life? Don't you think that if a man wants to be with someone more masculine than himself that he would just pick another man? And to be honest, I know in my own experience that when I was in a relationship with someone who was less masculine than I, I lost all respect for that person. In my first marriage, I was the masculine one, and I had zero respect for my ex-husband. My friend, the one I told you about who told her boyfriend what to order when we went out to eat, lived in the masculine energy. You might think I'm being stereotypical, but I'm sharing my experience and what I've noticed in others. It's more than a role we play; it's a way of being that aligns us with your true natures.

Did you read the quote at the beginning of the chapter? It's worth repeating. Lao Zi said, "Water is the softest thing, yet, it can penetrate mountains and earth. This shows clearly the principle of softness overcoming hardness." Living in your feminine energy doesn't mean you become a pushover. Ask anyone who knows me, and he or she will tell you I'm far from a pushover. But I have learned, through mindfulness and meditation, how to just *be*—how to step into flow, how to allow and accept. Once I moved to this place of allowing, I felt that the world opened to me.

It was at this point in my life that I met my husband Michael. When we first started dating, I was completely aware that I needed *him* to be the masculine one in our relationship, so I chose to take my masculine energy down a notch. Michael lives in his masculine energy. I know that if I go at him with the same masculine energy, we will have a war. Relationships need polarity. Think of the yin-yang symbol with darkness and light, hot and cold, and masculine and feminine interwoven and working together in unison.

Even though I was very aware of these energies, I still struggled with the transition from control to flow, moving from masculine to feminine energy. As my awareness of the two energies increased, I started to recognize that I could wear my tool belt of strength and power to work, but I was allowed to take it off when I got home. I knew from the past that there wasn't room in our relationship for two men (me and him). So when I got home, I relinquished to him masculine energy and I moved into flow. Part of being in flow means you are open to receiving. Sounds easy, I know. But if you are honest with yourself, I bet you will find that you are always busy doing for others and aren't used to anyone doing anything for you.

I remember that before we got married, Michael offered to make me an egg sandwich. I said, "Sure" until I realized he was making it only for me. He wasn't actually hungry. I said, "Wait. What? No. You can't do that." This was unheard of—someone doing something *just* for me. I was so uncomfortable with him doing so that I insisted that I could make it myself. I realized I was very uncomfortable with anyone serving me or doing something just for me. Because my relationship is so important, I prayed that I could embrace my feminine nature. I didn't want to chance that I would slip back to my old ways of control and harshness.

I had neglected my feminine energy for so long that the Divine had to step in and get my attention. Well, don't you know that God gave me the opportunity to practice living in the feminine, another teachable moment in my life? In April of 2016, I was in a CrossFit competition with my friend Nicole; we were doing the final workout, and I wasn't doing too badly (a.k.a. I wasn't losing). While doing "toes to bar" (a gymnastics movement where you hang on a bar and pull your toes up to touch the bar), my hand slipped, and I fell off the bar. I dropped about five feet with my feet in the air and landed on my right arm with it fully extended. Yikes! I dislocated my elbow, and I had to go to the hospital. There they knocked me out and had three grown-ass men pulling on my arm to put my elbow back in place. My arm was locked at a ninety-degree angle. The first few weeks I couldn't use my hand or lift my arm at all. I could barely wiggle my fingers. Months passed before I could bend or straighten my arm even a little bit. It took nine months of painful physical therapy to regain range of motion. By the way, I'm right handed, which means there were lots of things I couldn't do.

For the first two months, I couldn't wear my favorite tight jeans (I couldn't pull them up with one hand), wash my hair, cut my own food, tie my shoes, or put on deodorant. My poor husband had to help me with just about everything. He even tried to learn to put my hair in a ponytail. Talk about having to learn how to receive. I was learning the hard way.

The day after the injury, I was so depressed that I was focused on what seemed like a growing list of things I couldn't do. I was consumed. As an active person, not being able to do many of the things I loved was a challenging adjustment. Somehow, despite all I knew about the power of thought, I couldn't shift my focus. I knew I needed to do something that would help me make this shift. Sitting home and sulking wasn't working. To get out of my head, I went to this little spiritual store by my house called Solutions for Daily

Living in Newtown, Pennsylvania. I was hoping to find comfort, and I was trying to focus on the things I *could* do. While there, I went to get a cup of tea. I had my cup and got the tea bag set; then I realized I could pull the little thingy that dispensed hot water and hold my cup. With that, a lady slid beside me, took the cup from my hand, and filled it for me. I was overcome with emotion. How many times in my life have I deprived someone of the opportunity to serve me or offer a blessing? She was a blessing to me in that moment. And in that moment, I knew the lesson I needed to learn. I wasn't willing to let this learning opportunity pass me by. I also know that if you miss your opportunity to learn what God has for you, there is a good chance he may give you another opportunity.

Being in a sling didn't stop me from going to CrossFit. Two days after the injury, I went to work out. I basically just did a few squats and then just stood there, watching everyone else, because I couldn't do much more than that. But I showed up, and sometimes showing up is half the battle. While there my coach said, "Don't move." With that he reached down and tied my shoe. It was a very humbling moment that caused me to well up with tears. I began to see that in my daily life, I routinely refused to let anyone help me. *Ever.* This was a new experience for me. I cringed as I accepted the help. I was so uncomfortable. My response had always been, "Thank you, but I can do it myself"—until now, when I couldn't do it myself. I had begun to see that it was okay to let others help me. I always feared that letting someone help me was a sign of weakness. I have since learned that it's a sign of strength. Once I learned this, I became a better leader at work. I began to allow others to do things for me that I could easily do for myself. Allowing others to help freed me up to do cool things like write this book, and it helped those who worked for me to step up into a place of leadership.

Let's talk a little bit more about this feminine-versus-masculine energy. Your feminine nature is flowing, creative, expressive, and receiving. Your masculine nature is in control; it is the giver. We all have qualities of each, but getting back to your true nature brings harmony within relationships. Like I said, relationships need polarity. This is true for homosexual relationships as well. You can't both be in the masculine energy, and you can't both be in the feminine energy (well, you can, but you will probably both be miserable). My opinion is that there is nothing sexier than a man living in his masculine energy, and there is nothing more beautiful and sensual than a woman who fully embraces her feminine energy.

When you incorporate mindfulness into your life, you make space to become more aware of your true nature. You become more aware of these energies moving through you. It's also easier to notice when you aren't grounded, not living in truth, not present, and easier to pause when fear is creeping into your life.

Chapter 7

Embracing the Struggle

— ⚘ —

If there is no struggle, there is no progress.

—Frederick Douglass

I once heard struggle explained like this: it isn't on the mountaintop where we find growth but in the valley, where it is dark and murky. You may celebrate on the mountaintop, but nothing grows there. It's in the valley where you find all the nutrients you need. Dr. Wayne Dyer used to say that enlightenment follows suffering.

While in my graduate program at the University of South Florida, I remember the professor saying that the journey is the destination, meaning that life is about what you are doing in the moment. It isn't about the end goal; it's about how you get there. Are you enjoying the journey, or are you rushing to get to some imaginary finish line? Well, let me assure you that right now in this moment, you are exactly where you are supposed to be. This includes all the ups and downs. My life has been full of mountaintop experiences, but I have also spent a lot of time in the valley. Looking back, it seems that from the age of sixteen to my midtwenties, life was a real struggle. People saw me as incredibly strong. What they didn't see was me crying myself to sleep at night. I think we have theme songs for different periods in my life. Back then the song "The Warrior Is a Child" by Twila Paris was my theme song. I doubt you know this oldie, but it totally reflected how I was feeling. I felt like I was seen as a warrior, but I was really just a frightened child hiding behind my armor and crying on the inside. Twila Paris speaks about the idea that even those who may win the battles they are facing can suffer wounds in the process.

No one knew this, but I wore an armor of protection to hide the brokenness inside. My armor did nothing to protect me from pain and sadness. It only kept me there longer. I was hiding my pain from others. I was fighting—fighting to keep my head up, to keep going, to appear to have it all together. I was a lost child, struggling and broken.

I believe my personal transformation started maybe around the age of forty years old when I finally chose to stop being a victim, when I started taking responsibility for my life and my decisions, for my relationships and my joy. That was when I finally decided to remove the armor I hid behind.

Several years ago, my theme song changed to "Fight Song" by Rachel Platten. In this song she proclaims her power to overcome and fight. That was me. I was a small boat on an ocean, trying to send big waves into motion. Today I use my voice, and I have taken back my life, and you can too. I can't tell you exactly how to get there because your journey is uniquely yours. All I can do is share my journey with you and some of the strategies I used to alter the course of my life.

Today my personal theme song is "Champion" by Carrie Underwood. I can totally relate as she sings about being a soldier and living for the battle. And if I get knocked down, I will get up again because I am a champion. Any interest in joining me in becoming a champion? In becoming invincible, unbreakable, unstoppable, unshakeable? Well then, you are going to have to loosen the tight grip of control over your life and every situation. Remember when I told you about my prayer to God, when I woke up and said, "Hey,

God, how about you lead today, and I will follow"? That's when my life changed. I found that when I led and expected God to faithfully follow, things didn't turn out so well for me. The doors of my life opened when I relinquished control, when I was open to being led, when I moved into flow and dropped the resistance. My one friend sings "Jesus, Take the Wheel" when things get tough as a reminder that "I can't, but he [God, the Divine, whoever your higher power is] can." Did you hear that? "I can't, but he can."

Remember when I talked about staying busy as a way to avoid feeling the pain in my life? Ever notice that you feel uncomfortable in silence? Ever wonder why that is? Is it possible that in those moments of silence we have to face our fears, get real with ourselves, and actually get in touch with our true feelings? Instead of processing and dealing with our emotions, we stuff them in and hold those negative feelings within the cells of our being. That pain eats away at us when we don't allow it to move through us. We unknowingly trade emotional pain for physical pain. Emotional pain that is undealt with manifests itself in aches and pains in our bodies through chronic fatigue, depression, upset stomachs, headaches, and even cancer and heart issues. You may have heard it said that disease is "dis-ease" within your body.

I believe greatest challenge associated with meditation are the silence and the awkwardness of having to sit with ourselves. What would happen if you surrendered to that silence? What would happen if you allowed yourself to feel?

Do you remember what I said about negative feelings being like trash? Stuffing feelings is like stuffing too much garbage into a garbage can. Eventually it won't all fit. Things will start to get messy. They may start to stink, with a smell others will notice and want to avoid. They may start to spill all over the floor, all over your life. So maybe it's time to take the trash out, the emotional trash.

We are so used to numbing our pain. We look for anything that will distract us, anything from staying busy to engaging in sex, drugs, and alcohol. Some people stay consumed with their kids' lives and try to live vicariously through them to ease their personal pain. We do whatever it takes to distract us from our pain. We have become a society of the numb, drudging through life.

Years ago, I was called to the house of a family who had just found their son dead in his bedroom, overdosed on heroin. At the time my cousin was just a few months clean and sober, and living with me. I made my cousin come with me to the house because I wanted him to see the effects heroin use has on families. I wanted him to see the reality of addiction. I wanted him to feel the pain and suffering caused by addiction. At the house, my cousin stood in the same room as this young man's parents and grandmother. As they brought the body down in a body bag, the mother passed out, and then the grandmother passed out. Paramedics worked on them while trying to get the dead body out of the house.

The pain and anguish of the family were palpable. My cousin stood speechless. Later that day, he just kept saying, "I feel [pause], I feel [pause]." He had no words for what he was experiencing. He was used to numbing his pain with drugs and alcohol. It had been years since he felt intense feelings. Feeling had become foreign to him. I helped him by putting some feeling words to the experience and explained that it's okay to feel. I reassured him that though what he was experiencing was painful, it wouldn't kill him. I believe we all need to learn to feel again. I reminded him that he didn't need to turn off the feelings or numb them. It's okay to cry.

Somehow as we grow up, we learn to stuff all emotions, all our feelings both good and bad. If you grew up anything like I did, you may have been told, "Don't laugh" or "Stop crying." I know I was told both. I had learned to show as little emotion as possible. What I came to realize is that it's okay to laugh and cry. In fact, I now encourage both. When you work in the addiction field, unfortunately, you see a lot of people relapse and come to us upset and with lots of regrets. Cassie usually comes to me, saying, "Erica, [insert name] is out there crying."

And I say, "Good. She should cry."

I know that sounds totally cold and mean, but my point is always that it's a good thing when others are crying. I'm more concerned when they aren't crying, when they aren't feeling. I can work with someone who is feeling. I can't help a person who is cut off from all emotions. Some say we should welcome discomfort in our search for truth.

Today I was out on my paddleboard, trying to soak in the last days of warmth before the colder weather hit. While out in the harbor, a couple of boats passed by, leaving a significant wake. The first big wave to reach me dropped me to my knees. While kneeling on my board, contemplating getting back up, I realized it wasn't the wave that had made me fall. The wave wasn't the problem. *I* was the problem. Instead of paying attention, staying present and grounded, and feeling my way through the situation, I was still focused on my destination. I was trying to fight the wave and force my way to a place where I felt safe. I was trying to power through the moment. I was trying so hard to get out of my situation that I almost ended up in the water. I was trying, fighting, and paddling through the wave instead of riding it until it passed. I realized this was my old pattern for dealing with challenging situations in my life. There are times when the waves (or challenges) come into my life, and how I react to them determines the outcome. If I fight the waves, ignore them, or keep paddling despite them, I will lose my balance and fall right into the ocean. If I slow down, breathe, calmly feel the waves, bend my knees, and move with the wave, I can ride it out till it passes. Sometimes in life we are so busy trying to fix problems and stop the waves from coming that we lose our balance and fall into bigger problems. Sometimes we get hurt, and sometimes we just get a little wet.

Think for a second about a riptide, which is a current of water that flows from the shore and out to sea. Many people drown when they get caught in one of these currents because they panic, desperately try to swim back to shore, and get exhausted from the fight. Hopefully, everyone knows that you cannot swim against this current. To escape this fast-moving water, you must stay calm and swim perpendicular to the shore. If you're not a good swimmer or don't have the energy, it's recommended that you simply float on your back and go with the flow until the current dissipates. The moral of the story is, stop fighting and embrace the struggle.

One thing I have learned is that struggles give us an opportunity to learn and grow. I also learned that I don't need to fight life and resist struggles. These lessons are sometimes uncomfortable and painful. Earlier I mentioned that my therapist wanted me to "feel" rather than impulsively end the relationship I had no business being in in the first place. This was one of those valleys or growth moments for me. I had to stop working so hard to keep myself emotionally protected, guarded, and controlled.

As the days passed and I waited for that right moment, I used the time to do some soul searching and rebuilding. I had to rediscover who I was and what made me happy. During that time, I didn't fight the emotions. I stopped trying to change him and focused on changing me. I shifted my attention and focus to what I needed to change within me to become the person I wanted to be, the person I knew I could become, the person I *needed* to become. I needed to find my voice and figure out who I was.

The process took a little while, but I knew the time was right. The opportunity arrived for me to speak my truth and get out of the relationship. I knew what I needed to say without wavering or second-guessing myself. It wasn't a fight; I didn't blame him. I just needed something different. I know that had I been impulsive, I would have said things that led to a fight. I would have second-guessed my decision and may have ended up right back where I started. When all was said and he left, I had such joy, peace, and confidence that they were a little surprising. And what I told my cousin about feelings was true. I was painful and uncomfortable, but I didn't die. I see now that I needed that time to strengthen my wings.

Let me help you out with a better visual of what I'm talking about. I came across this parable years ago that talks about a man who finds a butterfly struggling to get out of a cocoon. He felt bad for the little guy, so he decided he would help it out by making the opening a little bigger. Then the butterfly wouldn't have to struggle. The only problem was that when the butterfly came out, its body was swollen with its wings shriveled. That butterfly spent the rest of its life crawling on the ground, never able to fly.

The man was trying to help the butterfly have a smoother transition from cocoon to freedom. He was trying to save the butterfly from having to struggle, but in his haste, he failed to realize that the butterfly needed the struggle to grow and develop its beautiful wings. Through the struggle the butterfly needed to push all the nutrients from the body to the tips of its wings. Instead of seeing a beautiful butterfly ready to soar, he had a chubby-bodied creature with puny wings that wasn't able to live the life it was supposed to.

Sometimes the process of growth starts with the struggle and ends with a soaring spirit. Once I left the struggle of my cocoon (the relationship), I was ready to soar. You will learn more from your struggles than from your successes. Don't fear the struggle. Years ago, Oprah Winfrey interviewed Will Smith about the making of the movie *Karate Kid*, staring Will's son Jaden Smith. In this interview, Will talked about how difficult and dangerous some of the scenes were. I will never forget what he said. "Greatness lies on the brink of disaster." That quote has always stuck with me as being true in my own life. Just when I feel like I'm going to lose everything, remarkable things happen. But the situation requires trust and faith that you are going to be okay. And if you ever doubt you are going to make it through the latest crisis, look back on your life, and you will see all you have been through. You will realize it's just part of the journey, and you will get past this challenging moment just like you did with all the challenges that came before this one.

It has been said that if something doesn't challenge you, it doesn't change you. What matters most is what you choose to do with the challenges in your life. If you need examples of how incredible lives are created from great hardship, read Viktor Frankl's book *Man's Search for Meaning* or read about the lives of Oprah Winfrey and Eminem. If you know their stories, you know that some would say they were dealt a bad hand. If you had known them as children and understood their struggles, surely you would have thought both Oprah and Eminem didn't stand a chance. The odds against them were too great to overcome.

Learn to weather the storm and know this moment is but for a season. Remember the expression "This too shall pass." Know that you will come out stronger on the other side. Struggles are just opportunities to learn. As we get older, we forget how to learn—I mean to really learn something like when we were kids. Remember when you learned to write in cursive. As adults we shy away from anything that requires completely new learning; we pause at the thought of developing new skills. We like to stay with what is familiar, so we stick to studying different variations of what we already know. We like to avoid mistakes, but true learning requires mistakes.

The book *The Talent Code* says struggles aren't optional, but they are a neurotically required process of mastering skill. You must make mistakes and pay attention to those mistakes.

Allow yourself to make mistakes. We aren't looking for perfection. There is a fine line between trying hard and being perfect. Striving to be perfect leads to frustration, depression, and a desire to give up.

As I mentioned in the introduction, I love to learn. To challenge myself, I decided to take guitar lessons. And wow, was that a challenge. During my first lesson, the guitar teacher gave me the following simple instructions:

1. Put your hands in place.
2. Play the note.
3. Relax.
4. Reset.

Seems simple, right? Not for me. Not for the one who has a natural tendency to rush things and speed through life. He kept reminding me to play slowly and said the only way I could learn to play the guitar would be to play slowly, relaxed, and ready to rest. The same is true for life. We can rush through life, making mistakes without correcting our actions. This pattern leads us to continually make errors and prevents us from mastering our craft.

The guitar teacher told me I must play the guitar with love, that I must seduce the guitar. We must slow down and embrace the struggle. How would things look if you played the game of life with love and seduction?

Consider this excerpt from *Think and Grow Rich* by Napoleon Hill: "Remember that all who succeed in life get off to a bad start and pass through many heartbreaking struggles before they 'arrive.' The turning point in the lives of those who succeed, usually comes at the moment of some crisis, through which they are introduced to their 'other selves.'"

Chapter 8

Breaking Rules

—⑤—

True learning comes from unlearning.

—*A Course in Miracles*

"**Y**ou'll get your heart broken. You'll get hurt. You will never make any money doing that. You'll poke an eye out." While trying to protect us, our family and friends have inadvertently taught us to play small, and too often they have killed our spirits. Some of us have learned to stay safe by not taking chances.

In the book *The Answer: Grow Any Business, Achieve Financial Freedom, and Live an Extraordinary Life*, John Assaraf says that by the age of seventy, most people have heard the words "You can't" one hundred fifty thousand times and heard the words "Yes, you can" only five thousand times. So think for a minute—how many times have you heard the words "You can't"? Have they translated into the belief that you can't? For me they did. If you are anything like the old me, you say the words "I can't" way more often than "I can." How do you think these words have shaped your life? How often have you squashed your hopes and dreams with the words "But I can't"? For example, "I would love to own my own home, but I could never save up for the down payment," "I wish I could lose weight, but I just can't," or "I would love to own my own business, but I just can't." We develop a limiting system of beliefs.

As Assaraf says, the habit of thought is more powerful than any desire. And often this disempowering language or thoughts have become habits. And they guarantee that our thoughts become things. What we think and say becomes self-fulfilling. It becomes our reality. To be free, we must take a closer look at why we do what we do.

I remember hearing the story of a woman who cut the ends off her pot roast and threw them away. Her daughter asked her, "Mom, why do you cut off the ends?"

The mother explained, "This is the way my mother taught me to make a pot roast."

The girl was very curious, so she went to her grandmother and asked, "Gram, why do you cut the ends off the roast?"

Her grandmother said, "Because I had a small pan, and I had to cut the ends off the roast to make it fit."

Isn't it crazy how often we do things just because that's the way it has always been done? There is an ancient story of a young student who went to visit the spiritual Master of his town. He asked, "Master, teach me all that you know about life." Before answering, the master got two cups of water. He explained, "This cup is what I know, and this cup is what you know. For me to share my knowledge with you, you must empty your cup of your own opinions and speculations. How can I teach you anything unless you first empty your cup?"

I have found that I need to take a close look at both my beliefs and actions, and then evaluate what I am doing and why. It's so true that we sometimes need to unlearn certain things. I have needed to empty my own cup. I had to unlearn the pronunciation of certain words. When I was growing up, my mom's English wasn't great, and she either butchered words or just said them in Italian. There were certain words I didn't even realize were Italian. For example, I didn't know that the thing you use to strain spaghetti is called a "colander." I thought everyone called it a "scolapasta." In grade school, I had a teacher named Sister Mary Agnes, and my mom called her Sister Mary Onions. When my mom complained about how messy my room was, she said it looked like a tomato (tornado) had hit the place. And she was worried about getting old and developing "author-asthma" (a.k.a. arthritis or "old-timers," meaning Alzheimer's).

Sometimes when learning or even unlearning, it's helpful to find a coach or mentor. A coach can help you identify areas that need to be learned, strengthened or "unlearned." This is often true for me at CrossFit. I find lots of parallels between my life and what happens in the CrossFit box. (CrossFit has its own language. They don't call it a gym; they call it a box). CrossFit involves Olympic weight lifting as well as intensive cardio training. I love all of it, but I especially love weight lifting. When I practice a lift, I'm practicing with the intention of lifting a heavier weight; I want to do better than I did last week. This is similar to how in life I am practicing doing more and better. An untrained eye may watch me lift 110 pounds over my head and be impressed, but an experienced coach, with his or her trained eye, may look at me and say, "You muscled through that. Your form is off. Redo it." Then he or she will identify where I went wrong and recommend what I need to do differently. When your form is off, you will get to a point where you can't lift any more. You can no longer muscle through the lift. You are limited by your poor form. More importantly, lifting with poor form can cause injuries.

Much like life, maybe we appear successful, but if our form is off, we struggle and muscle through. We may need someone more experienced or highly trained to point out small tweaks that need to be made to help us achieve success with greater ease.

Not one of us exists in isolation. We need people in our lives to help us. One of the biggest lessons I have learned from CrossFit is that we can't let our egos get in the way of our learning and improving. I have learned that sometimes we must take some of the weight off, take a step back, and practice some of the basics. That happened to me today. My form was off, so rather than pushing through and putting more weight on the bar, I backed off, grabbed a PVC pipe, and just practiced my form. I had to relearn how do that particular lift. When I take the advice of a coach, I see improvements.

When learning a new skill or seeking information about something we have no knowledge of, it can be helpful to work with others. Enlisting the help of a coach can help you find the areas of your life where limiting beliefs are holding you back. I personally have worked with various life coaches over the years to help me dream big, set goals, hold me accountable, and identify areas in my life that need a little work. They help me strategize how I can get from where I am to where I want to be. My coaches help me identify limiting beliefs that still creep in despite the work I have already done. It is through this work that I have come to realize the impact of the rules I have developed for living. They weren't always the rules others placed on me that held me back; they were often my own rules, rules I had created to achieve my false sense of security.

Let me ask you, Who would you be if you let go of the rules others had created for you? What are the rules or beliefs others have created for you that don't resonate with your true self? Here are some of the rules I held on to. These are the rules others placed on me and the consequences they had on my life.

Rule: Do as you are told and never question authority.

Consequence: I obeyed without questioning. I did what others told me to do, even if I didn't agree.

Rule: Self-expression isn't okay

Consequence: I lost my identity. I made sure I looked and sounded like everyone else.

Rule: Don't show emotions.

Consequence: I stopped laughing, hid pain, and became numb. I built walls of protection. I locked everyone out of my life. I put on a mask.

Rule: Act proper and show restraint. Or act like an adult.

Consequence: I stopped dancing and singing. I stopped playing.

Rule: Be modest. Don't be sexy.

Consequence: I learned to hide my body. The feeling of shame became a norm. I didn't know how to live in my own skin.

Rule: Be humble.

Consequence: I accepted less than I deserved.

Rule: Once married, you must stay married at all costs, because divorce is a sin.

Consequence: I stayed miserably married for eleven years and totally lost myself.

Rule: Don't draw attention to yourself.

Consequence: I became muted. I hid and tried to make myself invisible.

Rule: Be strong.

Consequence: I became a bulldozer and tried to power my way through life. I never allowed myself to be vulnerable enough to let anyone help me.

Rule: Don't take risks because you'll get hurt.

Consequence: I never tried anything new. I played safe and small.

When I took a closer look at the rules others had created for me and the rules I had created for myself, I was left to question my identity. Who am I once you pull away all the rules and restrictions that others put on my life? What would I do differently? Would I try new things? Act silly? Would I have fun? Would I laugh more? Would I be more comfortable in my own skin?

Would I dare to go to a nude beach? Would I wear a sexy dress because I like how it looks on me and how I feel when I wear it? Would I have sex freely without holding back? Would I dance like no one was watching? Would I know and embrace who I really am? What would my life look like if I were free to be me? If I were free to express myself? Free to take chances?

After years and years of living by everyone else's rules for us, we often lose sight of who we are. I once attended a One World Academy meditation retreat where the spiritual leader told the following story:

> There once was a woodcutter who lived in a small village. He was content living a simple life, living in his small house, with not a lot of possessions. He liked his life, but he had a secret obsession; the golden eagle. For he had seen a golden eagle in the woods. He was fascinated by the golden eagle and he wanted to catch him and keep him for his own. But as you know, it is not easy to capture a golden eagle. The woodcutter followed the eagle and he tried and tried to capture it, but every time he would get close, the golden eagle would fly away. But one day while in the woods, he found a nest with golden eagle eggs. The woodcutter took one of the eggs and placed it to hatch with one of his chickens. So, this baby golden eagle hatched with the baby chicks. He did not know that he was a golden eagle. He believed that he was a chicken. He even acted like his siblings.
>
> Growing up, this golden eagle would look up in the sky, sad that he could not fly like the other birds. So, he went to his mom and asked her to

teach him to fly. His mom said, "You are not a golden eagle, just give up you are nothing more than a chicken. You are not a golden eagle." His mom loved him, but she believed that he was a chicken and she wanted to protect him.

One day, an eagle swoops down and picks up the baby chicken, looks at the little guy and says, "What are you doing down here." He responds, "I am a chicken." The eagle tells him, "You are not a chicken, you are a golden eagle" and with that he teaches him to fly.

Who is the "hen" in your life who has told you you can't fly? I know I had many hens in my life, mostly family members who told me, "You can't do that" or "Don't do that."

Now I ask, "Why can't I do that?" Now I'm not afraid to try. Now when I tell my family I am going to do something, I just get an eye roll. They know it's pointless to tell me what I can't or shouldn't do. My daughters don't know me to be any other way. I told my daughter I was going to write this book, and her response was, "Of course you are."

Who are you once you remove the label others have put on you? I know you're probably not into reading children's books at this point in your life unless you have little ones, but there are a few that are worth reading as an adult. One is a beautiful book called *You Are Special* by Max Lucado. This book tells the story of a character who is defined by the labels others have placed on him. The pictures illustrate others walking by him and putting little, round stickers on him. The main character doesn't believe he is good enough because of what others say about him. The book is a beautiful reminder that you are loved and beautiful just the way you are, flaws and all.

I think it's time to look at the labels others have put on you and the labels you have put on yourself. Look at the rules that define your life. Do these rules serve you?

Chapter 9

Speak Your Truth

—◦§◦—

Our doubts are traitors and make us lose the good
we oft might win, by fearing to attempt.

—William Shakespeare

Most of my life, I lived with the crippling belief that I wasn't smart enough, good enough, thin enough, pretty enough, or _____ enough. You could fill in the blank; I just wasn't enough. Living with the belief that I wasn't enough held me back from living, from taking chances, from believing I deserved more. It left me without hope that a better life was even possible. I avoided being vulnerable. I avoided being seen. I didn't want others to see what I saw, so I hid. I was hiding my weakness, pain, and unhappiness.

Charles C. Finn wrote a poem that struck home with me. I discovered this little gem when I was eighteen years old. Oddly enough, it was part of the employee packet I was given when I was hired to work at the psychiatric home. When I read the poem for the first time, I experienced a sense of relief. I felt like someone understood me. I felt like he was writing about me. He started the poem by saying,

Don't be fooled by the face I wear. For I wear a
thousand masks.

Pretending is an art that's second nature
with me ...

Beneath dwells the real me in confusion, in fear,
in aloneness. But I hide this. I don't want anybody
to know it. I panic at the thought of my weakness
and fear exposing them. That's why I frantically
create my mask to hide behind ...

I'm afraid that deep-down I'm nothing, that I'm
just no good and you will see this and reject me ...

Despite what books say of men, I am irrational;
I fight against the very thing that I cry out for.

I had built some pretty thick walls around my heart, hoping not
to get hurt. I later learned my walls didn't protect me but rather kept
me hostage to my pain. I loved this poem. As I read it at this point in
my life, I realize I'm at a totally different place in my life, and I can
no longer relate. I see that I was successful at removing the walls by
chipping away at them little by little. I had to do the work myself.
For years, I thought someone would one day come along and save
me, as if it were someone else's responsibility to help take down the
wall—someone else's responsibility to make me feel safe enough to
remove the mask.

I know many women who believe a man should be the one
to rescue them, that their own emotional state is their partner's
responsibility. But I have to tell you that you are your own salvation.
A friend posted this on social media: "Everyone has baggage, find
someone who loves you enough to help you unpack." I wanted to
scream, "Unpack your own damn baggage!" You don't need anyone
to help you unpack. In fact, no one *can* help you do the work. You
must do it yourself, and you must do it *for* yourself. You deserve to
be free from all that is holding you back. And freedom is possible.

It starts by figuring out who you are and being true to yourself.

Let down your guard just a little, and you will see that you are safe. You will find that the people will love you anyway, despite your flaws. Stop hiding. Know you are blessed. You are special. You are made in the image of God, and as they say, "God don't make no junk." I know this is easier said than done, but keep reading.

Pink says it best in her song "Fuckin' Perfect." She recognizes that we may feel misunderstood and underestimated. She acknowledges mistakes and bad decisions and says they're all right. She sings, "Please don't see yourself anything less than fuckin' perfect." So the next time you are in your car, play that song. Put the windows down, turn the music up, and sing—and remind yourself that you are perfect, mistakes and all.

It's time to shift your thinking that you aren't enough to thoughts that are more empowering. When you go about daily life, believing and feeling like you aren't enough, you put limits on what you can do, affecting every area of your life. Like thoughts, feelings become reality if not kept in check. When we stop hiding and start to own our power, great things happen.

In my life, there were real consequences for believing I wasn't good enough. That story kept me in bad relationships and caused me to make bad business decisions. Let me give you an example of what I mean. In 2012, I applied to be a substance abuse treatment provider in a drug and alcohol treatment center. I had no treatment experience. I had never been to treatment, and I had never worked in a treatment center, yet I felt like this was what I was supposed to do. I saw a need in my community, and this was my attempt to fill it. Not knowing anything about business, I was convinced I couldn't do this alone, so I brought in people as business partners and trusted them to lead the way. I didn't know it at the time, but these weren't good people, and they took advantage of my lack of self-confidence and experience. I trusted them too much and doubted myself. This situation cost me money and peace. I had to pay a lot of money and had to endure a lot of bullshit to get them out of my life. You would think that I would have learned my lesson the first time. Nope. For years, I felt like I walked around with a big bull's-eye on my forehead and a sign on my back that said, "She is easy to take advantage of since she does not trust her own judgment."

Believing that I wasn't good or smart enough, or that I didn't have enough experience in this field to be successful, I thought I needed the help of other people. I wore my vulnerability like a coat. So, what do you think happened when I met someone who said, "I know how you can grow more business and make more money"? Yup, I trusted this person. Again, I thought he knew better, that he was smarter, and that he could do what I couldn't. So I guess you wouldn't be surprised if I told you that he stole from me, contributed nothing, and caused my life to be a living hell. To end this nightmare and get him out of my life, I had threatened to press charges after he altered his paycheck by adding a couple of zeros.

Like I said, be thankful for the troubled times, for your teachers and all those great opportunities. As hard as these situations were for me to go through, I know I needed these experiences to grow and get stronger. Without these experiences, I wouldn't be who I am today. I am a strong, confident, and savvy businesswoman. I would have had to close the doors years ago had I not learned the lessons from difficult situations. I wouldn't have developed the confidence that comes from sticking up for myself and speaking my truth.

One of my great coaches taught me that to be happy, successful, and true to myself, I needed to honor my truth. And my truth is that I need to

- use my voice;
- stay true to my values; and
- follow my gut.

Your gut is like your internal GPS. You don't need to know the entire route; you just need to trust that it will get you there. Life has proved to me that when I honor my truth and do these three things,

I can't go wrong. When I look back on my life, I see how failing to do just one of those three things caused me a lot of pain.

Remember Ariel from the movie, *The Little Mermaid*? She traded her voice for legs. What have you traded your voice for? Did you trade your voice for the false sense of peace? Did you trade your voice for approval? Well, it's time to tap into that inner knowing. It's time to use your voice, stay true to your values, and follow your gut. It's time for you to recognize you are fuckin' perfect.

When my daughter was old enough to drive, I decided to give her my Honda Pilot and find a cute car for myself. I realized this was my opportunity to try something new, to shift from the belief that I wasn't good enough or deserving of good things to a belief that I was worthy and fuckin' perfect just the way I was. So I investigated getting a Mercedes. I found that I could lease one for less than the payments I was still making on my five-year-old Pilot. So, to embrace a new lifestyle and way of thinking, I signed the lease on a cute little Mercedes. I wish I could say I loved every minute of it, but truth be told, I didn't. Whenever someone said, "Wow, nice car!" I felt uncomfortable.

I would say, "I got a really good deal on it." I felt guilty. I was embarrassed to drive it, as if I wasn't good enough to drive a Mercedes. As I drove around, I was afraid I was being judged. The funny thing is that the only person judging me was me. And the judgment I feared reflected how I had judged others. I had to work on feeling worthy enough to be driving that car.

Previously, my ass-backward thinking had me sabotaging myself left and right. The negative beliefs that I had about myself did little to help me out in life. I had a strong belief that I was stupid. Remember, I mentioned that in my mind it was better not to try and fail than to give a shit about what I was doing—to really try and fail anyway. It was easier for me to say that I failed because I didn't try, because to try and still to fail would prove to me and everyone around me that I was in fact as stupid as I thought I was. From an early age, my beliefs and attitudes were shaping my life—and not in a positive way. I had developed unhealthy habits when it came to my way of thinking. I had to totally retrain my brain.

Most of us tend to have a script or recording that plays over and over in our minds. We relive painful experiences; we repeatedly beat ourselves up for mistakes we have made in life. We put ourselves down and hold onto limiting and negative beliefs about ourselves. Constantly saying to yourself, "I am not good enough," may be the most crippling of beliefs. I have learned that the two most powerful words in the English language are "I am." Anything we put after the words "I am" has the power to set limits or set us free. Proverbs says the tongue has the power of life and death. Buddha teaches that our thoughts shape us and that we become what we think. So watch what you say about yourself and practice new, powerful, and positive "I AM" statements. (Check out the "I AM" cards I created at my website, EricaMortimer.com.)

We often develop beliefs about different situations to make sense of our unpredictable, crazy lives. The problem is that beliefs don't equal truths. Sometimes it's our unhealthy beliefs that put us in conflict with truth and peace. Our beliefs about situations are typically made up of our feelings, what we think and maybe pieces of truth. I have had to learn to honor truth despite my feelings. I told my therapist, "I feel like I am [fill in the blank]."

And my therapist asked, "Is that true?"

There was a time in my life when I was so confused that I didn't know what was true and what wasn't. So my therapist had me map it out. In one column she had me write what I "feel." In the second column I wrote what I "think" about what I felt. And in the third column I wrote out what was "true." This little exercise helped me to sort out my feelings, thoughts, and actual truth in life.

What do you feel?	What do you think?	What is the truth?

It's funny that when you break things down, the awful ones you are feeling or maybe thinking conflict with the truth, yet we continue to hold on to these irrational thoughts. For example, I may have the belief that I'm stupid. So let's break it down. I may feel stupid, and think I can't do something, yet the truth is that I have already proved that I'm not stupid and have excelled in many ways.

I finally learned that I had to let go of the past and embrace the future. I had to divorce the story and marry the truth. While making this transition, I felt like I was stuck in the middle. I wasn't totally prepared to let go of the past. Yet I was struggling to move forward; I was grasping for the next ring, but I couldn't let go of the old one. So I stayed stuck for a while. It was through prayer, meditation, and learning to "slow the fuck down" that I was able to make the daring move forward, to let go of the past. When I learned to just "be," I was able to see more clearly. I was able to see how the limiting beliefs and self-loathing were hurting me. This realization made it easier to begin to rewrite the script that played in my head. I uncovered my true self, and I was finally able to speak my truth.

Chapter 10

The Power of Gratitude

———⚬⚭⚬———

The struggle ends when gratitude begins.

—Neale Donald Walsh

As I was learning to rewrite the rules for my life, I had to rerecord the message that played repeatedly in my brain. I had to reprogram my thinking. I bet you can guess one of my favorite techniques for reprograming my brain. That's right! Gratitude. Here was an exercise that helped me shift my thoughts and feelings about my own body. A friend challenged me to pick an area of my body I wasn't so fond of and write a nice or positive poem about that body part. I chose my thighs. After struggling to find anything nice to say about my thighs, here is what I came up with:

Ode to My Thighs
Unappreciated for much too long,
My thighs have proven to always be strong.
The power they possess can turn a few heads,
while carrying me up mountains,
Through life and even to bed.
They ride, climb, lift, and push on till they ache.

I push them so hard that sometimes they shake.

But my thighs are resilient, healthy, and powerful.

While always seeking the illusion of perfection, I failed to realize there was no need for correction. For my thighs say to the work that I am a woman.

They are clearly not the legs of a child, boy, or man.

I have lived a life supported by their strength.

So, starting today I will show gratitude and honor the gift of my legs.

They crave the sun, yearn to run, carry me on my journey,

And they have

NEVER LET ME DOWN.

I know this seems like a super-corny thing to do, but I share this poem with you because I wanted to show you one way to help you shift your focus to one that is more positive. So now, instead of saying, "My thighs are so big," I say, "My thighs are incredibly powerful." Sometimes I give my legs a little pat of appreciation and thank them for allowing me to do things I love. Since I wrote that, I have a greater appreciation for my legs and for what I have. I have a greater appreciation for their strength. Believe it or not, I have started wearing shorts, something I refused to do for many years. And all it took was a small shift in my thinking.

You may be starting to notice that negative thoughts and old stories have the power to shape our reality. We stack thoughts and stories, and they grow in power. Part of the challenge is to separate your feelings from your thoughts. So if your focus is on negative things, your feelings will match those thoughts. Likewise, if your thoughts are positive, your feelings will match those thoughts. Now stack negative thoughts on negative thoughts; you are guaranteed to feel like shit. But what if you had the power to stack positive thoughts in a way that made you feel energized, alive, and excited for what was to come?

The truth is, you have the power. Just like Glenda said to Dorothy in *The Wizard of Oz*, "You had the power the whole time, my dear." Remember, Dorothy was lost, and all she wanted was to get back home. Well, consider this: all Dorothy needed to do was face her fears and overcome the challenge in front of her to experience the power that was always within her. The same is true for you. You may feel lost, and you may be longing to get back to your emotional home, that place you used to enjoy when you were young and didn't have a care in the world—you know, before you felt like life had beaten you up. You have the power to go back there. The method isn't complicated. It may be challenging because many of us have gotten into the habit of negative thought patterns, but through quieting our minds and making slight shifts in our awareness, we will find that we can break the bonds that keep us stuck.

Consider this: how easy is it to break a piece of thread? Pretty easy, right? Well, what happens if you take that piece of thread and twist it with two or more strands of thread? It gets stronger. Now, how easy is it to break? The answer is that it isn't very easy. Thoughts are the same way. When you get into negative thought patterns and twist negative thoughts together, the feeling of negativity gets stronger and is harder to break. So here is my suggestion: raise your awareness around how you feel and how different thoughts make you feel. If you have a thought that doesn't feel good, start to switch paths. Change your focus. You don't need to break all the threads in one shot, just one at a time—and gently. Here is an example for you. You are in line at the grocery store, and the lines are long, and the line you pick doesn't seem to be moving. You get to pick thought pattern A or thought pattern B. As you read the two options, notice how each dialogue makes you feel.

Pattern A

What is wrong with this bitch?

Why is the cashier moving so slowly?

She doesn't know what she is doing.

I have things to do. I don't have time to stand in line all day.

Oh my God! I can't believe the lady in front of me. Why does she need fifty packs of ramen noodles?

Bitch, let's go! I can't wait to get out of here.

It's getting hot in here! Great. I'm sweating. I will probably get sick. Thanks a lot, lady!

It's all your fault. Let's go already. Where the hell did you learn to bag groceries?

Pattern B

Wow! The store is really busy today. The cashier looks really tired. I bet she has had a rough day. Customers aren't always kind. When I get up there, I am going to see if I can brighten her day with a smile and maybe ask her how she is doing.

Oh wow, the lady in front of me has a lot of ramen noodles in there. Maybe that is all she can afford. I'm very blessed in that I have money in my wallet and can afford what is in my cart right now.

It's warm in here; I think I will take off my coat.

It's great that this store hires people with special needs to help with bagging groceries and helping customers. She looks like she is struggling a little. Maybe I can go help her while I'm waiting.

I felt a little stressed just writing Pattern A.

Have you ever been stuck in traffic and bitched and complained about being inconvenienced? Have you ever been stuck in traffic and considered that someone ahead of you may have been in a serious accident and may be fighting for his or her life? Doesn't that thought feel different in your body? My point is that you can always choose better feeling thoughts. One thing I know for sure is that gratitude always feels better.

As I mentioned, gratitude has been one of the most important tools on my journey to stillness, peace, and contentment. I mentioned that I work in a challenging industry, where people don't always do the right thing. I had a situation once where someone with a lot of personal issues got mad at me and wanted to cause problems for me. As a way to get even, the person accused me of insurance fraud, reporting me to every governing agency he or she could think of. As a result, I had to endure several long on-site investigations. One of these investigation lasted over four hours. To say I was a nervous wreck may be an understatement. I was beside myself. I asked myself, "How can this be happening? I always try to do the right thing."

Remember my Catholic school upbringing? Even as an adult, I was afraid of getting in trouble. I had never had to deal with anything like this. I kept thinking, *I am a good person, trying to help people. I haven't done anything wrong. Why do I have to go through this?* When the investigators first showed up, I took a deep breath and told myself, *I did nothing wrong, and it will all be fine.* I tried to stay positive. After the first hour of them being in my office, I was struggling to keep it together. I had to rely on the tools I had learned over the years. I know that *fear cannot exist in the presence of gratitude.* So I started finding things to be grateful for. I wrote what I was grateful for on a sticky note and put it up on the wall. Into the second hour of the investigation, I just kept telling myself, *They will be finished soon,* and that I just needed to stay in gratitude and take nice, deep breaths. Into the third hour, I was fighting tears. I was also fighting the thought that I could lose everything I had worked so hard to create.

When those negative thoughts crept up, I acknowledged them and just said to myself, *That isn't true,* and I let that thought pass through. In the third and fourth hours, I was struggling to find things to be grateful for, so I started asking people around me what they were grateful for. I wrote their response on a sticky note and added it to the wall, which we later referred to as the "wall of gratitude." It was something I kept in place until I had to change offices. I was able to sit back and see all the great things I had to be grateful for in my life and in the lives of others.

Once the four-hour investigation was over, I was told the accusations were unfounded and that everything was in order. I believe that creating my gratitude wall kept me from losing my mind that day. There is power in gratitude.

I have also found the practice of gratitude critical to overcoming my own sloppy thinking. I know we have the power to choose better feeling thoughts. So if you don't want to turn into an angry bitch, shift your focus and choose a better feeling thought. Side note: anger doesn't look good on anyone.

Chapter 11

Sloppy Thinking

———⟡———

Your mind is a garden; your thoughts are the seeds.
You can grow flowers, or you can grow weeds.

—William Wordsworth

As adults, we have a tendency to gravitate to negativity. We like to revisit failures and find wrong all around us. Our conversations tend to be fear based; they tend to be about failure, wrongdoing, or sickness. Sometimes if you listen to other people's conversations, it is as if they are having a competition about who is in more pain, whose job is worse, and whose life sucks more. I'm competitive and like to win, but I don't want to win that game.

There was a time in my life when the idea of shaping my thoughts was a foreign concept. I was a sloppy thinker. I was a victim of my brain. Thoughts got stuck in my head, and I couldn't get past them. And I probably don't need to tell you that these thoughts were neither uplifting nor positive. They were usually self-loathing in nature. I would beat myself up for days over something stupid I had done or said. These thoughts had a direct impact on my mood, motivation, and how I interacted with others. These thoughts kept me hiding and put a wall between me and others.

It's hard to strive toward good things in life when you're constantly beating yourself up. I also couldn't move forward, because I was always stuck in the past. As I mentioned, when I learned to slow the fuck down and get quiet, I became much more aware of what was going on in my brain and the types of thoughts that raced through there. With an increased awareness, I was able to put the brakes on thoughts that didn't serve me. I began to consciously choose to let them pass through as a train at the train station. Picture yourself standing next to the tracks. You watch the train pull in, but you realize it isn't headed in a direction you want to go.

You have a choice in the moment either to get on the train or to wait for the next one. You don't get mad at the train for pulling into the station. You just say, "Hey, that isn't the direction I want to go today. I will let this one pass. Maybe I will get on the next one if it is headed in the direction I want to go." And then you do nothing. It's the same thing with your thoughts. You don't need to entertain every thought. You don't need to hold it tight and dwell on it for days. There are times when a thought pops into my head that doesn't serve me—fear, for example. Rather than attach myself to the thought, I just say to myself, "Nope, I'm not riding that train," and I let that thought pass on by.

Years ago I read a book called *The Secret* by Rhonda Byrne. If you haven't read it, I recommend that you check it out. It's an easy and fun read. It was while devouring this book that I learned about the power of thought and the law of attraction. As I studied and learned more about the law of attraction, the more convinced I became that I needed to gain control over the three-ring circus taking place in my head. But I guess I should back up in case you haven't read this little gem of a book. Byrne and the teachers she highlights in the book describe the Universe (you can even think of God or any other name that suits you) as a great genie. Think of the genie from *Aladdin*, except instead of getting only three wishes, you get unlimited ones. The catch is that it's your thoughts and the things you focus on that act as your wishes. And those wishes (thoughts) then become reality. So if you're sloppy with your thinking, you will end up with a mess. Remember, the genie always has one response. "Your wish is my command."

The same is true with the Universe. When you complain or focus on the things you don't want in your life, this is like asking for more. The Universe doesn't differentiate between "want" and "don't want." It's all about energy and the feelings you attach to each thought. It has nothing to do with your words. If you are complaining or focusing on what's negative, the Universe says, "Oh, you want more?" *Bam!* Now things really suck. So let's break it down. Thoughts become feelings, and feelings become things. The Buddha taught that you become what you think.

Let me give you a few examples. Have you ever bought a new car, then suddenly you saw the same make and model everywhere? Or have you ever thought of a friend, then suddenly had him or her call or show up? How about that morning when you stubbed your toe while getting out of bed? You cursed and said, "Great! This is how my day is going to start?" Then your entire day went to shit.

You have the power to shape your day, life, and destiny with the power of your thoughts. I know this may sound really hocus-pocus, but it's not. The law of attraction is just as real as the law of gravity.

Can you imagine how foreign this concept was for me at first? Remember, I always used to be prepared for the worst-case scenario. My fucked-up thinking kept giving me more of the same grief I was hoping to avoid because that is what I was focused on at all times. I was always focused on what's negative. I always noticed what was wrong and rarely noticed what was right. It was like I was always trying to get ahead of the problem so there would be no surprises.

To be honest with you, the former version of me was a judgmental bitch. I had spent most of my life being critical of everyone and everything. I judged everything as either good or bad. But to be honest, I was focused mostly on the bad. I was quick to point out what was wrong to anyone who would listen. I could tear someone apart in two seconds and point out all his or her flaws. I didn't discriminate; I did this to everyone, including myself. To be honest, I was even harsher with myself. I was very negative about life in general. This perspective makes for a miserable existence. I don't know how anyone could even stand to be around me. When you live like this, there is no reason to smile. This may sound weird, but when I was single and out in the bars, men walking past me said, "You should smile." This didn't happen once or twice. This happened a lot. I mean, come on. Perfect strangers could see how miserable I was. What's funny about this is that at the time, I thought I *was* smiling. I guess I had a "resting bitch face" and didn't even know it. Melancholy and miserable were my norm, and they apparently showed on my face.

In 2014, I attended Tony Robbins's event called Date with Destiny (fun fact: I actually attended the event featured in I Am Not Your Guru). It was at this event that Tony challenged us to find what was right in life. I started paying attention to my critical judgments of others and myself. I realized I never found anything good, because I was so busy actively looking for what was wrong. For example, if I threw a party, I was more focused on who didn't show up rather than on appreciating and enjoying the company of those who did show up.

As I noticed where my focus was, I realized I had to make some changes. I started practicing finding what's right. I seriously had to practice. This wasn't something that felt even close to natural for me. I had to work at finding things to appreciate. I would sit on a bench, watch strangers go by, and try to find something positive about them. For example, I saw a crazy looking lady go by with the most ridiculously colorful outfit; and rather than thinking, *What the hell was she thinking going out in public like that?* I had to learn to reframe my thinking. I had to put the brakes on my thoughts. I would literally make a screeching-brake sound to myself as I shifted my thinking. The conversation in my head started to go like this: *Look at that crazy bitch with … errrrrrrrr … nope … I mean, it's really great that she has the self-confidence to be that bold.* I'm not going to lie; this change took a lot of practice. I had to learn a whole new way of thinking. I had to practice finding what was right about the situation and stop myself from constantly seeking what was wrong. It was a choice I realized I could make. I realized I didn't have to be a victim of sloppy thinking any longer.

One of the greatest lessons in my life came from Brother Dennis at Notre Dame High School. He was the softball coach during my sophomore year of high school. I was trying out for the team and was actually pretty good, so I was shocked when he cut me in the first round. I really had no idea why I had been cut. A good friend was also trying out for the team; she couldn't even catch the ball, and she made the team. I was so puzzled that I thought maybe there had been a mistake. It wasn't in my nature to question authority, but because I was so baffled, I mustered the nerve to ask him why he had picked someone who couldn't catch over me. What he told me was shocking. He said I had been cut because I had a bad attitude and all I did was complain.

I was shocked. I was a good kid and didn't mean anything by the things I was saying. Looking back, I realize that I did complain—a lot. I grumbled when we had to run and had a negative comment for everything. I went from "I can't believe he is making us run like this in the heat" to "This is so dumb." I didn't mean anything by my comments; they were just my way of making conversation, of being funny. It was my way of connecting with other people because I didn't know what else to say. At least that's what I thought at the time. I see now that being negative, grumbling, and complaining were a bad habit of thought and speech. They were simply evidence of my sloppy thinking.

I was completely unaware of what I was doing, but I wasn't totally wrong. Being negative and complaining are often the ways we relate and connect with others. Finding shared complaints is a great way for people to bond, to show they can relate and sympathize. Imagine this scenario: you run into an old friend and ask how he or she is doing. The person's response is, "Ah, not bad. My bad back is acting up, and I just missed work for a week because my kids were sick."

You may be tempted to respond by saying, "Yeah, my back has been bothering me too" or "My kids have been sick too. I bet they caught it from that kid Tommy."

Many people have a habit of matching the despair of the person they are talking to so they can connect and relate. I have learned that instead of matching their misery, I can simply say, "I am sorry to hear that," and then leave it alone or shift the conversation to something good. For example, what I do now is respond with, "You are so blessed to have health insurance that allows you to see a doctor" or "It's great that you have a job that gives you days off so you were able to stay with the kids while they were sick." I have come to realize that I don't like how it feels to be in a conversation with someone who only complains. Maybe that is why I disliked myself for so many years.

The old me knew only misery and grumbling. Oddly enough, I always seemed to be looking for more. I was always ready to point out something that was wrong. The first thing I noticed in any situation was what I didn't like or what I thought needed to be changed. My focus was on what was wrong about the situation, and it became the first thing I could think to talk about with others. I had to create a new habit. I learned that I had to ask better questions. I learned that I had to make a habit of asking, "What is right about this?" I began to change the words I used to reflect what is good. I'm not going to lie; there were many times when I had to bite my tongue to fight myself from blurting out something completely negative.

I know I get on my husband's nerves, but when we are in the car, stuck in traffic, he starts huffing and puffing and complaining about the traffic; then I start coming up with all the things that are right about the situation. I usually say, "There might be an accident ahead. I am grateful that our family is safe. Isn't it great that our heat or air-conditioning works so we aren't uncomfortable while we wait? We should probably pray that no one is injured up ahead." This shift in thinking was helpful in my quest to find things to be grateful for. It's easy to find peace and calm when you're grateful. It's hard to find things to be grateful for when you see only what is wrong in your life. And it's hard to feel good when you see only what's bad.

One day I was walking my dog through our nice suburb; my neighbor's weeds made me feel better about the weeds in my own yard. We all do this from time to time. We look for weeds all around us to help us feel better about our weeds, circumstances, bodies, relationships, even our performance. We often look to find fault with others but to feel better about ourselves. When I catch myself doing this, I must immediately stop myself and find what's right, what's good, or what is going well. Don't get wrapped up in the weeds of your life or the weeds in someone else's life. It isn't worth your time. It isn't worth the consequences that follow. Plus, remember the law of attraction. Unless you want more of the same, you better knock that shit off. Focus on the weeds, and you'll just get more weeds. Those weeds may come in different forms, but they are guaranteed to come. It's the law, the law of attraction.

The law of attraction says that "like attracts like." Simply put, think good thoughts, and more good things happen. Think bad thoughts, and more dreadful things happen. In other words, thoughts become things. Thoughts with matching feelings become very powerful. There are those who say we manifest all that comes into our lives. We are co-creators of our reality. And we do this creating with our thoughts. Proverbs 4:23 tells us we should both guard and protect our minds because from them flow life.

I'm hoping you will be able to see the difference in the way I dealt with thoughts before and how I deal with, manage, and view thoughts now. This is all possible because I became quiet. Once I was quiet, my awareness increased. I could hear myself, feel what was happening, and make the constant small shifts in thinking. Today I can find joy, peace, and gratitude in just about every moment. Some moments are more difficult than others, and sometimes I get off course. Sometimes I feel out of alignment, out of balance, and ungrounded. I don't beat myself up about not being at my best. I now know what I need to do to get back to a place of joy. I know I need to "slow the fuck down," take a deep breath, and redirect my attention. I have to shift my thoughts to ones that offer a higher vibration, to those that simply feel better, thoughts that bring me closer to where I want to be. I don't like the way anger and anxiety feel, so I choose to move away from those feeling. I'm not saying you shouldn't feel negative feelings. I'm just saying that you don't need to hold on to those feelings with a death grip. Let that shit go.

Challenging moments are part of life. They offer contrast. Abraham-Hicks says we need contrast in our lives. It is contrast that helps us appreciate when we're in alignment. In case you aren't familiar with the name, Abraham-Hicks is the cocreation between teacher and author Esther Hicks and an energy she refers to as a group of nonphysical entities or a group consciousness from the nonphysical dimension. Abraham has said, "We are that which you are. You are the leading edge of that which we are. We are that which is at the heart of all religions." Their teachings are inspiring. They encourage readers and listeners to embrace what they wish to create and acknowledge their connection to Source energy or what many refer to as God.

We tend to forget or neglect our connection to God. One of my favorite things to do it to listen to Abraham recordings whenever I can. Instead of watching television while you fold clothes, listen to one of these recordings. You can find many great recordings on YouTube. One of my very favorite things to listen to is Esther Hicks's recording on YouTube titled "Everything Is Always Working Out for Me." This is my go-to recording when I want to shift my thoughts and feelings. Sometimes I like to listen to this before I'm about to fall asleep.

When you do have a negative thought (or thoughts) that don't serve you, you don't need to beat yourself up over it. Just acknowledge the thought and move on. That thought isn't yours to hold on to. Philippians 4:8 tells us to think about that which is true, noble, right, pure, lovely, and admirable. And if anything else is excellent or worthy of praise, we should think about these things.

One of the things I used to do early in my journey was to set the alarm on my phone to go off several times a day. When the alarm went off, I did a self-check. I asked myself the following:

- Where is my focus?
- What am I doing with my body?
  - ○ Am I sitting or standing in a way that is empowering or defeated?
- What kind of language am I using?
  - ○ Are my words uplifting? Or are my words filled with venom?

One thing I do to help me practice shifting my thoughts is to keep a Gratitude Journal. I already talked about the importance of an "attitude of gratitude" and how it has helped me gracefully navigate tough situations (okay, maybe I didn't do it all that gracefully, but that is how I choose to remember the story). My Gratitude Journal has helped me practice finding feel-good thoughts. I like to do a big ol' gratitude brain dump. I dump everything I can think of to be grateful for on the page. This is especially helpful when you're not feeling good about something. Maybe there's something in your life that's causing you some fear or anxiety. Maybe you're having a tough time shaking that feeling or shifting those thoughts. That is an appropriate time to do a gratitude brain dump around the issue.

If you want to take it to the next level, talk about it with someone. It's important to note that you aren't talking about the problems but all you are grateful for. You don't even need to give the back story. I have a friend I can do this with. We talk about what we are grateful for and the great things we are experiencing. We even brag. We even randomly say to each other, "Give me a brag." We focus on the things that make us feel good, the things that give us pleasure. If a thought creeps in that has some emotions that don't feel good, we make the shift. It's easier for me to think of it in terms of gratitude rather than just thinking positively. Positive thinking is good but not as powerful as gratitude in shifting the feelings attached to the thought.

I'm not saying that if you think only positive thoughts, your life will be grand. Positive thinking isn't going to turn the weeds in your front yard into lilies. Your grumpy husband won't suddenly become a jolly fellow. But what I am saying is that you can dramatically improve the quality of your life and the joy you experience if you focus on what's positive, what is going right; focus on the things in your life you want more of. And do this no matter what is going on around you. Hey, there is always room for a good old sob fest. Get it out, let it go, and shift. Don't stay there. Choose to feel good; choose joy. As you do this, you will find that your husband isn't as grumpy as he was. Or maybe he is, but you just don't notice this trait anymore because your focus has changed.

I'm certain that as you make the shift, people will react differently to you. Just think—how do you feel when you meet someone who looks angry, with eyebrows bunched and fists clenched? How about when you meet someone smiling with arms wide open to greet you? Don't you react differently to each of these people? Aren't you warmer and friendlier to the person who appears to be happier than to the one who appears to be miserable? The same will happen to you. You will find that people you meet become nicer; you will find people want to help you. The best thing I have experienced since my personal shift is that cashiers offer me discounts, even when I don't ask. Score!

If you're struggling with how to get started, I suggest you start by celebrating little things. For example, my shoes are really comfortable, and I'm so grateful that there is food in my refrigerator and that my bills are all paid.

Chapter 12

Discovering Self-Care

—Ⓢ—

An empty lantern provides no light.
Self-care is the fuel that allows your light to shine brightly.

—Author Unknown

Self-care is a foreign concept for most people. I mentioned earlier that I had to date myself for a month. It wasn't until I was pushed to do this activity that I saw just how badly I had treated myself. Self-care wasn't something I had considered. I'm not sure I saw that value in self-care or even self-kindness.

Many of us are great about taking care of everyone around us, but we stink at taking care of ourselves. No matter how often we hear about self-care, we tend to ignore the recommendation. We make excuses for not taking care of ourselves first. We like to say we don't have the time, money, or whatever to take care of ourselves. Despite warning signs that it's time to slow down, look within, and practice self-care, we continue on with life as if nothing is wrong. This reminds me of a certain person I know, who shall remain nameless (cough, cough, Michael); he ignores every light that comes on in his car.

I say, "Hey, your fuel light is on."

His response (as we are passing a gas station): "We are fine. We can drive another thirty miles like this before we run out of gas."

I point out, "Your check engine light is on."

He says, "That light always comes on. It's fine."

No, it isn't fine! If the check engine light is on, you need to check the engine. If your fuel light is on, it's time to stop and get gas. What the fuck are you waiting for? It's not a suggestion. It's needed. Besides, isn't it more inconvenient for you to run out of gas than to just stop and fill the tank? Isn't it more inconvenient for your car to break down on the way to work than for you to schedule a tune-up? See what I mean. You are no different. Are there signs in your life that you need a tune-up? Are you stressed? Depressed? Overwhelmed? Feeling alone? Do you feel stuck? Then it seems your check engine light is on, and maybe you should look under the hood to see what is going on before things get worse.

When I started on this journey, I had no money or idea what self-care could look like. I thought self-care meant you treated yourself to massages or facials. Don't get me wrong—massages can be part of your self-care regimen, but they aren't all there is that you can do for yourself.

Sometimes self-care means stopping to put the oxygen mask on yourself before helping others. My husband recently suffered a heart attack and had to undergo open heart surgery. The first few days were incredibly stressful. I brought him to the hospital on a Wednesday night; by Thursday evening, he was in surgery. By this point, I had been at the hospital for nearly thirty-two hours with no sleep or shower, and I'd been eating only crappy hospital food. The food was so bad that I just kept thinking the hospital was using the cafeteria to drum up more business for itself. My brother-in-law had a cheesesteak sandwich that looked more like a shredded, wet, brown napkin sandwich.

Michael's surgery was supposed to take up to four hours. This was my window to force myself in those critical moments to practice self-care in whatever way I could. So, despite not wanting to leave the hospital, I ran home for a quick shower and fresh clothes. In those moments of stress, I knew what I needed. I was gone for about forty-five minutes, but when I got back to the hospital, I was still stressed, worried, and extremely tired; but at least I didn't smell, and I was able to worry in fresh clothes rather than in the sweaty, stinky ones I had been wearing.

When my husband was discharged from the hospital, I knew I needed to continue to practice self-care in whatever way I could yet still be there for him. Since I wasn't comfortable leaving him home alone, I had to find ways that didn't involve my leaving the house. In addition to sleep and showers, I knew I needed to eat nutritious meals. That first day home, I created a menu for the week of healthy meals. I ordered my groceries online and had my daughter pick them up from the grocery store. I took care of myself (and him) by eating foods that would fuel my body. I took my vitamins and drank plenty of water. This may not sound like much, but in times of stress, we often forget to do some of the most basic things. What is it that you need? Are you neglecting to take care of yourself because you are busy taking care of someone else?

If you grew up like me, you may have been taught that there is honor in being a martyr. I now know that isn't true. And I am telling you that you are more useful to others if you take care of yourself, if you fill your internal gas tank.

Sometime self-care means setting boundaries with others; maybe it means sticking up for yourself. One of the most empowering things I ever did for myself was fighting back and sticking up for myself. I earlier mentioned the guy who accused me of insurance fraud and reported me to insurance companies, sparking a frivolous investigation. Well, this same guy harassed me endlessly. In addition to calling every insurance company, accusing me of fraud, he called the state ethics committee, saying I was involved in unethical practices. He did everything he could to have my licensed revoked and tried to have me shut down. He sent me horribly mean and threatening e-mails several times a day. Not only was he harassing me, but he was harassing my staff as well. All allegations were unfounded, but he still didn't stop harassing me. I was losing sleep and worried about what he would try next. I was paranoid and started looking over my shoulder. I knew he was on a mission to destroy me.

There was a time in my life when I would have just gone into hiding, given up, and just taken whatever abuse came my way. I would have just prayed for the trial to end. But being a stronger and more empowered person, I filed a police report. People tried to get me to drop everything, saying nothing would come of it, but I insisted on following through with the legal action and making him as uncomfortable as he made me. In the end, I didn't win in court, but I won the battle. He finally left me alone. He knew I would take legal action and refused to back down. For me this was a small personal victory. For the first time in my adult life, I stood up for myself and refused to be a victim.

Look at those in your life. Are there people who don't have your best interest at heart? Do you have some "frenemies"? You know, those "friends" who would love to see you cut off at the knees? Are there people who would simply like to see you stay stuck with them? Do they resent your successes? Maybe it's time to set some boundaries. Break ties with those who may be dimming your light. Rumi once said, "Set your life on fire. Seek those who fan your flames."

Another form of self-care is tending to your physical needs. Do you need to get your ass to the gym? Then do it. You can find really cheap gym memberships these days. If you aren't comfortable going to the gym, check out some of the great phone apps that walk you through workouts you can do at home. Aaptiv is a great one. Have you ever thought about running a 5K but don't know how to get started with running? Check out *5K Runner: Couch Potato to 5K*. Or maybe you want to start with something gentler. Check out the Down Dog app. It's like having a yoga instructor in your back pocket.

Aside from working out, there are other things you can do that take little effort but may have a big effect. I'm not into makeup and would prefer to not wear any, but sometimes it feels good to fix myself up a little, even if I'm not going anywhere. When you do things for you and not for anyone else, you are practicing self-care. When you do something that brings you joy and pleasure, you are practicing self-care. When you do something that makes you smile, you are practicing self-care. What can you do for yourself today that would make you feel good? How can you fill your internal gas tank?

You may not have considered this, but how about offering forgiveness? Have you considered offering forgiveness to yourself? Are you beating yourself up for past mistakes? I bet there are others in your life whom you need to forgive as well. Holding a grudge and anger serves no purpose. Maybe you have heard this saying: "Holding a resentment is like drinking poison and waiting for the other person to die." Or this one: "Resentment is like pissing down your own leg; you're the only one who feels it, but everyone else sees it."

Remember earlier when I talked about the women with the pursed lips, tight shoulders, and furrowed brows? They have bitterness written all over their faces, just like I once did. Have you ever seen a child with these features? Of course you haven't. Children haven't had the years of experience that come with this special look. The look doesn't develop overnight. It takes years of holding on to old hurts and resentments.

The Bible says we need to become childlike to enter heaven, that he who humbles himself as a child will be the greatest in heaven (Matthew 18:3–4). Let's look at some of the qualities of children.

- They are free to express themselves and don't pretend to be something or someone they're not.
- They don't hold back. They dance, skip, sing, and say what they want or need.
- They aren't afraid to make mistakes.

- They aren't troubled or held back by the past.
- They don't worry about the future.
- They aren't concerned about what others think of them.
- They don't keep a record of wrongs, meaning that they don't hold on to resentments.

If we would live with these traits, don't you think it would be a little like heaven on earth? If you are living in the past, you are living in untruth. My favorite meme is "Let that shit go, homie." If you are living in the past, you are being limited. Living in the past limits creativity and spontaneity, and it limits you from forming new and great relationships. Can you see how forgiving others can be a form of self-care?

When you offer forgiveness to someone else, this isn't really even about the other person. You aren't forgiving the person for his or her benefit. You are forgiving the person for *your* benefit. How free would you feel if you weren't burdened with the weight of past hurts? I know there are people in your life who have really hurt you, and you may not see how you can forgive them. I hear you saying, "But Erica, you don't understand how bad they hurt me." And I'm saying that it doesn't matter, because right now you are allowing them to keep you in a victim role. Do you want to continue to feel the sting of their actions, or are you ready to heal? If you want to heal, you will need to forgive.

I know this may seem trite but keep in mind that hurt people hurt people. Maybe you can write that person a letter. Say what you have to say, then burn the letter. Remember the quote from earlier. "No man is your friend, no man is your enemy; every man is your teacher." As the saying goes, people come into your life for a reason and a season. If someone hurt you, I guarantee there was a lesson in there you were supposed to learn. My experience has taught me that if I don't surrender to the lesson, I'm doomed to repeat the experience. That guy I told you harassed me endlessly came into my life to teach me something. I'm embarrassed by how long it took me to learn the lesson. If I'm being honest, I must admit that he wasn't the first person to bully me and try to hurt me. But he sure was the last. I learned what I needed to, and I moved on. I didn't hold a grudge, but rather I thank him (in my heart, not in person) for making me stronger. I offered him forgiveness, even though he never asked for it, may not have deserved it, and most likely wouldn't have even cared if I'd forgiven him. I did it for me, not for him.

If you are struggling with offering forgiveness to someone in particular, consider repeating the Ho'oponopono Prayer. *Ho'oponopono* means "to put right." It's a powerful way to release resentments toward others and self. This ancient Hawaiian practice of forgiveness uses the power of the words "I'm sorry. Please forgive me. Thank you. I love you" as a form of mental and spiritual cleaning. It is considered to be a means to cleanse the "errors of thought." It's similar to the Buddhist techniques used for clearing karma. Here is how you can use the process:

1. When you are in your meditation space, think of the person whom you are having an issue with. Maybe it's someone with whom you don't feel alignment.
2. In your mind's eye, see the other person.
3. Imagine Divine love flowing into your body from above. Picture this love overflowing.
4. Release this person and picture him or her floating away
5. Now when you think of that person, repeat the following as many times as you need to: "I'm sorry. Please forgive me. Thank you. I love you."

Sometimes it helps to keep in mind that most people are doing the best they know how. That includes you. I have found that the hardest people in our lives to forgive are ourselves. What is the tape playing in the background of your mind? Is it a song of guilt and shame or maybe fear and doubt? Tenth Avenue North has a beautiful song called "You Are More." This song acknowledges our shame, pain, and fear that we aren't enough. What the group says is that "you are more than your choices and more than your mistakes."

It's true; you are more than the mistakes of your past. It's time to release your guilt and shame. It's time to empty the junk drawer of your life. We all have a junk drawer, that dark out-of-the-way place where we keep all the useless stuff we don't want to throw away, but we also don't want anyone else to see it. It's time to get rid of the junk. But wait just one second. I know you. You are going to be tempted to analyze everything before you release it. *Don't do that!* Just fuckin' let it go. Let me give you a little visual. If you have a cat and you are changing the litter, do you inspect every piece of shit before you put it in the trash? For the love of all that is good, I hope not. That's gross, and it serves no purpose. No good will come from your analyzing all the junk.

I know what you're saying: "This is all well and good, Erica, but how the hell do I forgive myself?" Remember, in the chapter about meditation, I told you about the loving-kindness meditation. Well, that is what you are going to practice. But let me break it down for you in a little more detail.

For far too many years, my life was like Johnny Lee's song, I was lookin' for love in all the wrong places. I was looking for love outside of myself. I should have been looking within. Here is what I do when I need to work on self-love and self-forgiveness: First, I have a piece of rose quartz I put in my pocket. This crystal is used to attract and keep love. It also calms and heals the heart. Then I close my eyes, take a few deep breaths, and focus my attention on my own heart and on love. I picture the love in my heart as a glowing light. I picture that light growing and expanding until it's all around me, as if I'm glowing. I feel the essence and energy of love. I embrace love.

So let's recap some of the ways of offering yourself self-care. There are things as simple as drinking water and making healthy meals; then there are a couple of more challenging tasks, such as setting healthy boundaries and offering forgiveness.

Here are more ideas for self-care:

- Take a bath. If you have lavender oil, put a few drops in the hot water.
- Take a nap.
- Find a Reiki practitioner and schedule a session.
- Buy yourself a bouquet of flowers or even just a single rose.
- Get coffee with a friend.
- Take a few minutes to meditate.
- Here is a fun one. Assume what is called a "power pose." I like to imagine myself wearing a cape and standing tall like Wonder Woman. Stand as if you were about to take over the world.
- Pull out (and use) that great-smelling body lotion you never use. But don't just slap it on in a hurry. Put it on slowly, admiring every inch of skin.
- Take a few deep breaths. Breathe in for a count of eight. Hold it for a count of four and then exhale for a count of four. Do these breathe exercises four times.
- Make a homemade face mask. Here is a recipe:
  - Mash one-quarter of an avocado in a small bowl.
  - Stir in one tablespoon of cocoa powder and one tablespoon of honey, mashing and mixing well.
  - Apply the mask to your clean, dry skin for ten minutes.
  - Wash off with warm water, then moisturize as per usual.
- Take a dance break. Put on your favorite song, turn up the music, and just move it and shake whatcha mama gave you.
- Here is a good one. Turn down an invitation to hang out with someone who only likes to complain. I have a friend who would begin every phone call bitching about what was wrong in his life. Because he is a longtime friend, I felt free to tell him that in the next phone call he made to me, I wanted him to start by telling me all that was right in his life. He began to do that, and what do you know ... More

good stuff started happening. Is everything always cool in his life? Nope, but things are looking up.

- Move and stretch. If you don't have time for a whole yoga class, take five minutes to practice a few moves. If you have a dog, take him or her for a walk around the block.
- Sign up for a laughter yoga class. It's like internal jogging by using voluntary laughter. The way we breathe when we laugh mimics the deep, healing yoga breath. Don't worry, your body knows how to laugh, even if your mind isn't totally on board. Laughter is healing.
- How about this? Make an appointment for a physical. Or maybe you have done that and now have a script for bloodwork that has been sitting in the car for a while. Go take care of that shit.
- Oh, I know what you can try. Try doing some pleasure research. Yes, that's it! Do some research to see what brings you pleasure. That could be oh, so much fun. Pampering massage, a pole-dancing class, a decadent-food cooking class, a sensory-awakening exercise, a visit to an adult toy store, going to a day spa—the options are infinite.

I hope you see that self-care doesn't need to be expensive and time consuming. So now you have no excuse.

Chapter 13

Attract Your Tribe

———⟡———

You can't do epic shit with basic people.

—Author Unknown

Harvard studied seven thousand people over the course of seventy-five years to see what makes people happy and what keeps them living longer. The results of their study were clear. People's level of happiness and joy is directly related to the quality of their relationships. They found that the brain and body were happiest when making connections with other people. So this means that the quality of your life is directly related to the quality of your relationships.

Most of my adult life, I felt isolated and alone. I felt like I didn't really have any friends. I had a lot of acquaintances. I don't blame others for my loneliness. It was my own fault. I told you earlier that I wore a mask. I hid, and I built a strong wall around me, so of course I felt alone.

I also had a lot of people whom I felt I had been a great friend to, but they were by no means friends to me in return, probably because they didn't know me. Or should I say I wouldn't allow them to get to know me? (How could they? I didn't even know myself.) By that

I mean I was always there for my friends. I would drop what I was doing for them, and I would listen to their problems for hours on end. But I never felt they would do the same for me. I know, I know. I was so guarded and rigid that I made it difficult for anyone to get to know me. I know this now, but I had no clue back then. All I knew was that I felt alone.

Being vulnerable was something I avoided at all costs. Remember, I refused to ask for any kind of help. If by chance someone offered to help, my response was always the same: "No, thank you, I can handle it." I was always determined to "figure this out on my own." My attitude was, "I don't need anyone." As I began to work on myself, I realized a few things. I realized I needed to surround myself with people who were headed in the same direction. I needed people who wanted more out of life and weren't afraid to work for it. I also realized I needed to make relationships important again.

I had to make the choice to drop my bullshit story that I didn't need anyone. I needed to embrace the thought that relationships are important. I needed to knock down the walls, get real, and let people in my life. I also needed to give up the story that I couldn't be friends with other women. Yikes! Bet I struck a chord there.

For some reason, we as women have embraced this idea that all women are back-biting, catty bitches. It's like we have been programmed to hate each other. I remember being invited to events designed for women and saying, "Um, no thank you, I'll pass." No way did I want to be in a room full of all women. That sounded awful. That all changed for me in 2016 when I decided to try something different. I attended an event or program for women. This program spanned the course of several months and involved three hundred women gathering and allowing themselves to be completely vulnerable among each other. I had decided that if I was going to attend, I would play full out and embrace whatever was put in front of me.

I can't get into the details of this event, but I will say that it was very ... um, intimate. There was a beautifully orchestrated point in the program where most of the women were half or completely naked. The bravest and most confident among us actually strutted across the stage, completely naked, as the rest of us cheered them on. It was in that moment that I saw the most beautiful women I had ever seen. There were women of all different shapes, ages, colors, and sizes—and each and every one of them was beautiful. I also realized that the most beautiful thing you can wear is confidence. The vulnerability we each brought into the room made way for great relationships. We dropped the act that we had life all together and talked about real issues we all faced but no one ever talked about. It was all open to exploration and conversation—from sex, love, and intimate details about our bodies to the fear that we are somehow different (less than) the woman sitting next to us.

It was at this event that I realized I needed these strong, smart women in my life. I was then intent on finding my tribe. I needed a tribe of women I could walk through life with. Today I celebrate and am grateful that I have found my tribe. Their unwavering support and love have been life changing. And I'm excited to say that my circle continues to grow.

Hope you don't mind, but I would like to take a minute to brag about my badass tribe, my inner circle composed of women I turn to when I want to celebrate or need to cry. They are my sounding board, my encouragement, my advisers, my spiritual guides, and my inspiration. I am going to pick on Rania first, since she is the first official member of my tribe. I met Rania on the first day of the event I just mentioned. We met in line while waiting for them to open the doors. I thought she was crazy. As we stood in line, she told me about this guy who wanted to marry her, and as she did, she pulled an engagement ring from the bottom of her purse, showed it to me, and then threw it back in her purse in disgust. She explained that she didn't want to marry this guy or wear his ugly ring. She went on to explain that she had real problems, about which she didn't know what to do. Now remember, I am a counselor, and I have worked with thousands of people. I have heard just about everything—everything but this. Rania explained that her problem was that every man she met wanted to marry her, and this fact was really cramping her style. She had me cracking up. She was serious about this being a real problem.

Rania and I sat together most days of the event. As I got to know her, I found that we were completely different. She believed in open relationships, she embraced pleasure, she used the word *juicy* a lot, and she wasn't afraid to ask for what she wanted. She also knew how to show love to everyone she met. Rania never met a stranger. Not long ago, Rania and I were on a crowded subway in New York City when she made room for a young girl (in her twenties) to sit next to her. As the girl sat down, Rania put her arm around her and embraced her. I remember thinking, *She is crazy! This is New York! You can't just put your arm around the person sitting next to you on the subway. That isn't how people roll here.* By the time we got to our stop, the girl had her head resting on Rania's shoulder. They hugged, and we got off the train.

Just last week, Rania and I were enjoying another girl's day in New York. While shopping in the Nike store, the salesman told her he was able to save her money on the sneakers she wanted by giving her the online price. When she heard this, she quickly grabbed his face and kissed him on both cheeks. He didn't even see it coming. There is an openness about Rania I admire. I also admire the way she embraces life, seeks pleasure, and loves unconditionally. Not to mention that Rania is a badass who speaks five languages, is a single mom, and owns her own dance studio in Washington, DC. Her studio is called Jordin's Paradise, if you are ever in DC and want to visit. You could step out of your comfort zone, try a pole-dancing class or belly dancing, or take a class on how to give a lap dance.

Lindsay was the next member of my tribe. Lindsay and I met in the third month of the same event where I met Rania. Lindsay is another badass. She is a beautiful, confident woman who knows who she is and is clear about what she wants. Lindsay doesn't compromise. She isn't willing to settle for less. She is strong in her beliefs and isn't easily swayed. She has a deep understanding of spirituality, one that isn't limited by religion or dogma. She expands my thinking every time we talk. She is an entrepreneur. She has created her own line of all-natural skin care products called Shea Loves You. If you use shea butter and like the healing properties of essential oils, you will love her products. Lindsay and I can talk for hours about deep ideas, about how to move closer to God, and about how to manifest abundance. We talk about dreams, desires, and how we are going to take our lives to the next level. Over the years she has provided great insight, balance, direction, and friendship. Not to mention that Lindsay can throw a badass party. By the way, Lindsay is going to be famous one day—you'll see.

Next is Laurie. She and I crossed paths in the most random way, but the moment we met, I knew it wasn't a coincidence. I knew she was meant to be in my life. Laurie is a sought-after speaker who runs marathons, teaches physicians at an Ivy League university, and is owner of the McGarvey Group, which offers personal, professional, and corporate coaching. Laurie is one of the most intuitive women I know. She uses this intuition to keep me straight and point me in the right direction. Laurie is also my accountability partner. We speak every Monday morning at eight thirty a.m. to discuss our goals for the week.

I went from a person who thought she didn't need anyone to depending on the friendship of these three beautiful women. I went from having no friends to having the most amazing women in my life. My story doesn't end with Rania, Lindsay, and Laurie. I have other badass friends I count on as well. One of my badass friends is a doctor and also my hiking buddy. Another is a brilliant genetics geek I know I can count on for a competitive game of "What Do You Meme?" She also kicks ass at CrossFit and beach volleyball. Oh, by the way, the editor of this book is total badass as well. She has interviewed the most amazing people—I mean, really amazing people, including his Holiness the Dalai Lama. Edie and I met at a networking event. At this event we each took turns introducing ourselves. When it was my turn, I mentioned that I was writing this book. When I mentioned the name of the book, Edie said I had written it for her. She then asked whether I had an editor. When I said I didn't, she said, "You do now."

My dad tells me my grandmother used to have a saying: "*Chi va con lo zoppo lo impara a zoppare.*" Basically it means that if you hang with the lame, you will learn to limp. In other words, you become like those you hang out with. You know, if your friend says "ya'll," chances are that you might slip in a "ya'll" once in a while. One of my favorites is, if you hang out at a barbershop long enough, eventually you'll get a haircut.

What I am saying is, be selective about what you are exposed to. Look around. Where and how do you spend time? Who do you spend time with? Look left and right. Who are those surrounding you? Carefully select your tribe. Motivational speaker Jim Rohn tells us we are "the average of the five people we spend the most time with." We are both supported and influenced by those closest to us.

Listen, this doesn't mean you are too good to hang out with your old friends. It just means you are actively choosing the direction of your life. And unfortunately, sometimes we aren't headed in the same direction as those standing by us. One of the things I have learned to do through mindfulness and meditation is to feel. This time I'm not talking about feeling emotions. I'm talking about feeling moments, feeling energy, feeling your way through life. When I'm in someone's presence, I pay attention to the way I feel. You know, are you feeling good vibes or bad vibes? Just pay attention.

Years ago, I was involved in an activity developed by the US Coast Guard. We broke into teams, and each team was given a list of items we could have on a boat. We were to rank the objects in order of importance. Basically we needed to decide what would help us survive should we be lost at sea. First, we did this activity on our own; then we did it in our small group. We argued our case for why we thought it was more important to have the mosquito net versus the candy bar. As a team we had to decide how we would rank each item. The team list didn't look at all like my personal list. When the teams had their list settled, we were then given the correct answers. We were then asked to score both lists—the one we had created on our own and the list we had created as a group. Throughout the room, all the group scores were significantly higher than individual scores. What I learned that day was that we are smarter together than we are as individuals.

Make the effort to get to know new people. Go to new and different places. Try new things. I'm so glad that I let down my guard, stopped fearing rejection, and allowed room for these amazing women to enter my life. I'm so grateful for their presence and influence on me. I may not see them often, but we make time for each other and have the most meaningful conversations. Years ago, I didn't see it, but now I know it's important to surround yourself with good people. My tribe is helping to shape my life and helping me to become a better person. I dream bigger with them in my life. I believe together we can move mountains.

In closing, it's my desire that you be kind to yourself, move past fear, find the love you deserve, learn to live your truth, and ultimately learn to "slow the fuck down." Blessings to you. Namaste.

Printed in the United States
by Baker & Taylor Publisher Services